BONSAI

BONSAI

LINDA WALKER

JOHN GIFFORD LTD : LONDON

© 1970 *by Linda Walker*

First Published 1971
Reprinted 1975
Reprinted 1978

Published by John Gifford Ltd.
125 Charing Cross Road,
London, W.C.2

ISBN 0 7071 0282 0

Printed in Great Britain by
Biddles Ltd, Guildford, Surrey

Dedication

To my Family and J.H.L.

Acknowledgements

My grateful thanks go to my husband for the time he has given to helping me and for the photographs he has taken. My thanks also to Mrs. Valerie Young for her help and kindness and to Mr. Norman Gryspeerdt for the photographs of his beautiful trees.

Contents

List of Photographic Illustrations

List of Line Illustrations

1

Trees in Trays

Many years ago I saw a display of beautiful dwarf trees in a large store. The trees were forty and fifty years old and were enchanting with their appearance of age and evident health. Much as I wanted one I realised that I didn't have the vaguest idea of how to care for it and the thought of watching it die through ignorance was too much for me. With great regret I resisted the temptation to buy, but the seed was sown—the seed of determination to find out more about these fascinating little trees.

Bonsai translated literally just means—Trees in Trays.

The earliest type of potted tree was called 'hachi-no-ki', trees in pots, which distinguished it from 'hachi-ue', the potted plant. 'Hachi-niva' was a garden in a dish while 'bonkei' was a landscape on a tray, often with no plants. The growers of the trees in pots wished to distinguish between their dwarf trees and the multitude of potted plants, dish gardens and similar horticultural art forms; so the rules and traditions gradually isolated the art of dwarfing trees and it was called 'bonsai'—trees in trays.

It is thought that both the art of dwarfing and the containers used originated in China and possibly India but by the tenth century mention of bonsai is found in Japanese history. Illustrations of an even earlier period show bonsai displays on shelves. Writings produced since that time refer to the gathering of naturally dwarfed trees from the wild which were then made into bonsai. The process was gradual but the growing of the beautiful miniature trees that we know today interested an ever widening circle, spreading to America and Europe mainly since the last war.

It was natural that such an art form should grow up in Japan; their love of nature and miniature works of art linked with the contemplative philosophy of Buddha was fertile ground for the perfecting of this branch of horticulture. The evidence of the Japanese genius for the production of miniature works of all kinds is legion today and speaks highly for the patience and manual dexterity which they display.

Fortunately, for those of us who admire bonsai, the art of growing these tiny trees can be learned. There is no mystery that anyone with a reasonable knowledge of gardening—or the will to learn—cannot understand. Trees of any size have certain basic requirements and to maintain healthy growth these must be satisfied. To buy for oneself, or for another, one of these small trees to be used as an ornament could end in disappointment if the owner had no knowledge of the growing habits of trees. They are not pot plants and cannot be treated as such. To attempt to grow a bonsai as one would a begonia or a geranium would, in time, bring failure. If the tree lived it would soon cease to be a bonsai as it was fed, watered and repotted in ever larger pots as befits a geranium or begonia. The technique of maintaining healthy growth while checking it sufficiently to retain the dwarf characteristics of the tree is a combination of commonsense and a knowledge of elementary biology and gardening.

A bonsai should be a perfect, natural tree in miniature. It may be one tree, several or a group planting. The mature bonsai should be a blend of balance and harmony producing a work of art. The beauty of the tree is the first consideration therefore it follows that the tree, to be beautiful, must be healthy. It must not be subjected to neglect nor deprived of water, air or nutritious soil in an effort to achieve dwarfing. No tree could survive such treatment and remain a thing of beauty, so, provided the aim of the grower is to keep his trees beautiful, he must apply his knowledge to growing healthy trees as well as dwarf trees.

A study of trees in natural surroundings will show an enormous range of shapes and styles of growth. The aim of bonsai culture is to produce these natural styles in the small trees. The more grotesque of the styles are not as popular as they once were and most of the well-known masterpieces of the bonsai world have their full size counterparts in nature. Natural trees are shaped by conditions of soil, shallow or deep; the prevailing wind; accident, or conditions allowing perfect growth.

Early in the history of bonsai culture the trees were collected from the wild in Japan. Stunted and dwarfed by natural conditions the little trees were carefully taken up and re-established in containers of great beauty and, often, considerable value. Many of the now famous trees in Japan were gathered in this way and raised into the beautiful bonsai which have reached ages of up to two and three hundred years. An aged tree in the wild, or culti-vated as part of a park or garden, depends on nature for its needs and must withstand natural forces. A bonsai of the same age has been cared for by generations of skilled horticulturists and has been shielded from the greater hazards of wind and weather; its value is correspondingly high.

To the grower who is a novice it may appear discouraging to see a hundred year old tree hailed as a masterpiece, our life span

i and ii — Red Maple
    This fine Maple (also in colour on the cover) shows the contrasting beauty of summer foliage and bare winter branches. It has a recorded history of 129 years and was cared for by successive generations of one family for 71 years. At present the tree is 28″ high and has a 4″ trunk.

iii

iv

iii, iv and v — pp 5 and 6
    These three pines, photographed in their natural surround-
ings, indicate the origin of the bonsai styles.

v   Pines in natural surroundings

will not allow us to see our trees as mature as that! However the culture of these tiny trees is an intensely interesting hobby. Some may be discovered in the wild or in nurseries, others are grown from cuttings, seeds, layers or grafts, if one is sufficiently skilful. "To travel hopefully is better than to arrive", or, at least, in this case as good. After a reasonably short time, depending on the method of raising, it is possible to create an effective and artistic bonsai. As the tree takes shape and fulfills the decorative scheme planned it brings great satisfaction to the grower. Apparent age can be achieved with various techniques; the firm, thick little trunk develops and careful pruning shapes the tree, preserving the natural style while revealing the beauty of form to be found in trunk, branch, leaf and flower.

Many bonsai are evergreen and vary only a little as the seasons progress but others leaf, flower and fruit and, in due season, show the perfection of form in their bare branches. Wild cherry, with its small flowers, is much prized in Japan; crab-apple, where fruit succeeds blossom, is of constant interest; beech retains its brown foliage throughout the winter until the old leaves are forced off by the new, soft green growth of spring. So many trees, each with its own charm and interest, are available to the bonsai grower bringing pleasure in achievement and to the eye.

A certain understanding of trees, their habits of growth and form as related to the separate species, is helpful. Knowledge of growth habits, in particular, is useful when judging the suitability of a subject for bonsai. Although a species is not described as 'dwarf' or 'miniature' in the catalogues it may well be of a slow growing type that is admirably suited for our purpose. When buying from a nursery many trees described as 'slow growing' or 'suitable for the small garden' will prove useful for bonsai. With such a tree you have, so to speak, a head start! Many of the most

This is a raft planting of a Trident Maple and is reputed to be 70 years old. The apparent 'group' is grown from a single root of a seedling or a cutting and is 8″ tall and 18″ long.

Compare with a natural group
Compare the Maple with this natural group of willows.

vi and vii — Trident Maple pp 8
Imported in 1966 by Bromage and Young Ltd. from Fukukaen Bonsai Nurseries, Nagoya for Norman Gryspeerdt.

viii — Cotoneaster
  Imported in 1971 by Bromage and Young Ltd.
from Fukukaen Bonsai Nurseries, Nagoya, for Norman
Gryspeerdt.

The brilliant red berries of this cotoneaster provide interest
in the dormant season. This tree reputed to be about 30 years
old will have been grown from a layer or a cutting. The tree
is 16″ high and the trunk is 2″ across.

prized Japanese trees are grown from these slow growing species but they would not be dwarf if left to grow in the wild.

Trees vary so much at maturity, a slow growing tree takes fifty years to reach twenty feet while a swifter growing species may reach a hundred feet and more in the same length of time. Obviously the slower growing tree will present less problems and be easier to train.

When no description of the tree is available as, for instance, in a seedling from the wild or from the garden, it should be possible to trace the parent or, at least, a tree of the same species in the immediate vicinity. A little study of this tree will show the suitability of your find for growing a bonsai. The wide spacing between branches and leaves indicates a fast growing tree and, although this would be useful for gaining knowledge and experience, it will not be so suitable as the tree with branches placed close together.

Some species take on an appearance of age in a relatively short time either by reason of twisted growth, type of bark or roots which thicken early. For a tree to appear mature it must be in proportion, overlarge leaves or needles, large flowers or heavy, ill-proportioned fruit would immediately destroy the illusion of a mature, well balanced tree. So the choice must be carefully made; wild cherry rather than ornamental cherry, crab-apple before eating apple and pines with short needles rather than long. Some trees can be persuaded to reduce the size of their leaves considerably but there are others which will always remain out of proportion and they are best avoided.

Again, there are a few trees which do not thrive in containers and others which do not tolerate heavy pruning of either root or branch. These may be grown successfully by the expert but the novice would do well to start out with some of the easier subjects and graduate to the more difficult plants as his skill and knowledge increases.

Much assistance can be found, on the subject of the suitability of trees for bonsai, from some of the beautifully produced seed and plant catalogues. The short, apt descriptions can often be very helpful in deciding if the ultimate tree will be balanced and in proportion and a word or two as to soil preference, tolerance of sun or shade, habits of growth and so on can give an excellent guide as to the growing conditions required. Indeed, of late years, some catalogues are recommending species suitable for bonsai and a few nurseries undertake to supply small stock grown specifically for bonsai culture.

Bonsai is a branch of horticulture which combines practical knowledge and skill with artistic ability. Once interest in the subject is aroused it grows, and the 'one or two trees to try' become a large and varied collection which is always in danger of expansion. It is, after all, a pastime which has survived the centuries and is unique in that the same living plants have received daily care from many generations. These trees, treasured in Japan and displayed in the 'tokanoma'—the focal point of the room—return to us the quietness of thought that we have expended upon them and give a sense of peace and permanence of great value in our frenzied world.

2

Classification and Style

The appearance of a bonsai should be as natural as possible. The tiny tree should be reminiscent of others of its kind whose growth has gone unchecked. Complicated and much twisted forms which were once so popular are now much less so, indeed their main claim to popularity was that the spiralled or knotted trunk served to dwarf a sapling which had grown too tall. The trend now, however, is to present one of natures own forms. Observation of fully grown trees will produce many interesting ideas for training and they will all fall into one or the other of the accepted categories.

Although it is necessary to understand the classification of bonsai in the first instance it need not be regarded as a set of hard and fast rules. If a bonsai is balanced and artistic in appearance it will fall naturally into the appropriate class. With bonsai, as with other arts, ones' appreciation is heightened by some knowledge of the subject. A 'sunday painter' may never achieve the competence of an academician but understanding of the problems involved in the production of a finished work will add considerably to his pleasure on viewing a masterpiece. So it is with bonsai.

Bonsai are grown in a number of sizes. The large ones, which are usually over two feet in height, are mainly used for outdoor decoration. Standing beside a pool or on a patio or, as they may be used in Japan, to create a miniature landscape on a limited plot. Next in size come those trees between twelve inches and two feet in height. These, naturally, require less space for display but look best when standing alone, the attention should not be divided between two or more trees when they are used indoors. The most usual size of tree for indoor use is the little tree up to twelve inches tall. The mame bonsai are smaller again, the 'miniature miniatures'. These are usually under six inches high and are most suited to group display. Finally we have the very tiny trees, the 'finger tip' bonsai so-called because they can be carried on the tip of the finger. Usually one is drawn more to one size of bonsai than another but all are interesting and all bring their separate problems to be solved.

Bonsai in any of these sizes may also fall into one of the next two groups.

Ippon-ue—which is a single tree in a container.

Yose-ue—two or more trees planted in a container.

Sometimes it is necessary to look closely to distinguish between these two styles. Ippon-ue is a single plant in a container but it is possible for a single tree to have several trunks. In nature a tree may receive damage at an early stage and two trunks may grow where there should be one. Bonsai are to be found with a number of trunks, each being a variation of the Ippon-ue style. Tankan is a tree with a single trunk—the shape taken by the trunk is immaterial, again it can have one of several styles but the single trunk is tankan.

Sokan is a double trunked tree, one trunk usually being

13

1   *Ippon-ue, a single tree in a container.*

smaller than the other. The balance of the thicknesses of the trunks is important—one trunk being taller and thicker, the parent, than the other which represents the child. The trunks should divide close to the ground in all cases and thus they can be mistaken for yose-ue. The Japanese almost always use uneven numbers both in ippon-ue and yose-ue because, to them, odd numbers traditionally represent the idea of longevity and immortality. The Japanese word for 'four' is similar to the one they use for 'death' so a bonsai is never found with four trunks nor are four trees planted in one container. Sankan, gokan and shichikan are, respectively, three-trunked, five-trunked and seven-trunked.

Trees planted in the yose-ue style must show the beauty of the group rather than that of the individual. Group plantings can be varied in a number of ways; all the trees may be upright—as might be found in a beech wood; some might be upright while others, at the edge of the group, could be slanting outwards—

2   *Sokan, a double trunked tree.*

this may be seen in many naturally growing groups of pines. Again, all the trees of the group could lean in one direction suggesting shaping by prevailing winds. It is usual, in these group plantings, that each tree should have a single trunk and it is customary, also, to plant trees of one species, although occasionally this may be varied effectively by blending evergreen and deciduous trees. This is found in nature of course, but it needs great care to produce a natural looking bonsai of this type because it is essential that the whole planting should show unity of design.

15

3   *Sankan, a three trunked tree.*

The trees are planted collectively but must be considered individually when trimming so that the branches are thinned to prevent a muddled appearance and the separate trunks are shown.

4   *Yose-ue, two or more trees in a container.*

16

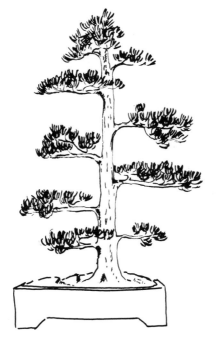

5   *Chokkan, an upright trunk.*

6   *Shakan, a leaning trunk.*

17

Primary branches should be separate but a little merging of the smaller branches may be allowed so that the foliage unites the group.

Further classification is now necessary because the shape and style of the trunk must be taken into consideration.

Chokkan, the tree with an upright trunk. This tree has a single tapering trunk, well placed and well developed.

Shakan, also a single trunk but leaning somewhat to the right or left, the branches being well grown on each side of the trunk. In nature such a tree would probably have been shaped by a light prevailing wind.

Bankan, this is a single, curving trunk bending in several directions.

Kengai, a cascading tree. This is one of the most difficult plants to display, a deeper container than that normally used for bonsai will help to balance the tree grown in this style.

Hankan, is a tree with a twisted, gnarled trunk which gives a weatherbeaten appearance and suggests a constant battle against hard, windswept conditions.

Ne-tsurani are, at first glance, yose-ue but examination will show that these seemingly separate trees are root-connected. Several shoots having developed from the same root it has the appearance of a group planting. It is, however, easier to care for than the group planting as the one root nourishes the whole planting equally and a more even appearance of growth is possible.

Ikada-buki, known as 'raft' bonsai, have a similar appearance to the ne-tsurani but in this case the trunk of the tree has been laid flat on the surface of the soil (or just below) and the branches, now rising vertically, have the semblance of a group planting. Again, however, this is a single planting or ippon-ue.

Lastly we must take into account the foundation from which the tree rises. The most usual base is the soil used in the container, it may be covered in moss, suitable alpine plants or small stones. This type of planting is easiest for a beginner and will almost surely prove a success. The various styles previously mentioned may all be grown in this way.

7   *Bankan, a curving trunk.*

A tree with an interesting root formation is often raised so that the root may be seen. These are known as 'neagari' and are much appreciated as the exposure of the gnarled roots helps to give the tree an appearance of great age. Some of the positions of the trunk are more suited to the exposed root style than others. In nature any tree that is windswept will, in all probability, also show its roots on the windward side. Similarly, a tree may have blown down and although the roots have pulled out of the ground somewhat, sufficient have remained for the tree to continue to thrive and the tree takes on the aspect of a raft bonsai or the

19

ne-tsurani style. Kengai represents the trees growing on the side of a cliff and in this instance the soil may have been washed from round the base of the tree producing, again, the exposed root base.

Ishi-tzuki has as its base a stone. This may be one tree or several planted on, or in the crevices of, a stone. The roots may

8 *Kengai, a cascading tree.*

be contained in a hollow of the stone or they may lead down to the soil in the container below. This is a very effective style but is more difficult to achieve successfully. Great care must be taken both in the choice of the tree and in the watering as well as in the initial planting.

20

Bonsai cotoneaster

Zelkova serrata (bonsai) in autumn

Once understood these classifications are not difficult to remember. Simply put, it is necessary to look for:—

The number of trees—one or several.

The number of trunks—single or multiple.

The stance of the trunk—straight, angled or cascading.

9   *Hankan, a twisted gnarled trunk.*

The foundation beneath—Earth, rock or exposed root.

When deciding the form of training for a bonsai the characteristics of the species to be used must be taken into consideration.

21

Each tree has its natural growth habit which is allied closely to its geographical position and environment. A tree that will grow straight and tall in a meadow will show multi-trunk or windswept styles at a higher altitude, the same tree at an even higher altitude could cling to the cliff face and become cascading.

10   *Ne-tsurani, root connected.*

Bearing this in mind it will be seen that one species of tree may be grown in several different styles and the resulting variation makes for increased interest and greater skill. Some trees are, of course, more suited to multiple plantings than others. For instance, flowering and fruiting trees are best used in a single planting whatever the stance or foundation. If a multiple planting is used it tends to detract from the beauty of flower and fruit. Pines and maples, on the other hand, are equally at home grouped together or standing alone. Trees that have a naturally twisted style of

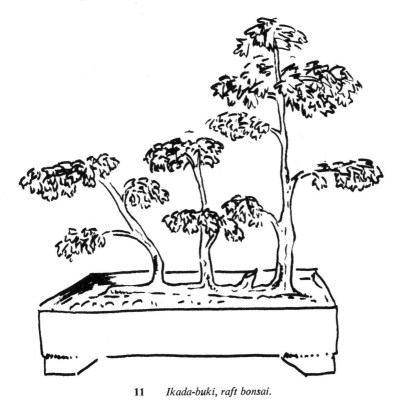

11   *Ikada-buki, raft bonsai.*

branch and root are also better in a single planting so that the form may be appreciated to the full. The same reasoning applies to the cascaded style, the beauty of the 'fall' would be lost if a multiple trunk or multiple planting were used.

23

An important point to remember when deciding on the style of a tree is that the tree must have a 'front' and a 'back'. The front should be the position from which the tree appears at its best.

12   *Neagari, exposed root.*

This is the position in which we will look at it and say 'this tree is in the sokan style' or 'the bankan style'. Whenever the tree receives attention of any kind it should be with the front of the tree in mind so that the style is not lost or altered but rather improves and is made more definite. If a sokan style tree was planted carelessly in its container the division of the trunk might not be shown to the best advantage. A good bonsai is one in which the front of the tree is quite obvious and care should be taken not to alter the position when replanting.

13   *Ishi-tzuki, based on a stone.*

If the general shape of the main branches and trunk of the tree is harmonious and balanced the rest will follow and the picture created will be both satisfying and artistic. The natural beauty of the tree must be the first consideration because it is nature that we are trying to emulate and to recreate in miniature.

25

3

Collecting and Propagating

There are three ways of acquiring bonsai. In the first place it is possible to buy one. This is getting much easier now, there are several firms who import them from Japan and there are nurseries specialising in rearing trees for bonsai.

To a novice it is very tempting to buy a 'ready made' tree where the picture is complete with moss, stones and suitable container. Or one may buy a tree 'root wrapped', that is, in its dormant

14   *Root wrapped tree.*

state with the roots free of soil and carefully protected by wrappings of sacking or raffia. Of the two I think the latter method is to be preferred for a beginner. It may sound as if the 'ready made' bonsai would be easier but if you have planted the tree yourself,

26

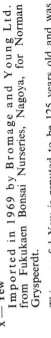

x — Yew
Imported in 1969 by Bromage and Young Ltd. from Fukukaen Bonsai Nurseries, Nagoya, for Norman Gryspeerdt.

This graceful Yew is reputed to be 125 years old and was originally gathered from the wild. The present height is 32" and the trunk measures 4" across.

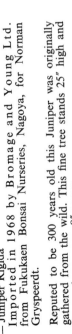

ix — Juniper Rigida
Imported in 1968 by Bromage and Young Ltd. from Fukukaen Bonsai Nurseries, Nagoya, for Norman Gryspeerdt.

Reputed to be 300 years old this Juniper was originally gathered from the wild. This fine tree stands 25" high and the trunk measures 8" across.

following instructions, you are not quite in the dark as to what is under the surface and, if all does not go well, a little checking up will probably point out the trouble. Whereas if you have bought your tree ready planted there is less chance of knowing if the drainage is insufficient or if the tree has run out of nourishment through being too long in the container.

However, I think a beginner would be well advised to try some of the other methods of obtaining trees because after a little more experience has been gained the care of a more expensive bonsai will not be such an anxiety and the chances of success are greater. It is as well to remember, if buying a root wrapped tree, that suppliers will usually only make these available after the end of October and before the end of April. During this period the tree does not make any growth and it is safe to package them in this way. Most suppliers will engage to send trees but the larger and older, and therefore more valuable, trees should really be collected from the nursery or importer to be on the safe side.

A visit to a nursery specialising in bonsai culture is very interesting, both to the novice and to the more experienced grower. Trees of all sorts are on display as are tools, containers, composts and stands. Probably the most valuable things to be found there are ideas! Ideas on how to improve your collection, add to it and display it adequately.

It is also possible to find a suitable subject for bonsai in an ordinary nursery or garden centre. Sometimes nurseries specialise in small plants while others insist on selling only well grown specimens. A nursery which will supply small plants is a great help as the tree can be trained without any of the drastic pruning which looks so ugly unless it is executed by a skilled hand. A little 'window shopping' at your local nursery will produce a suitable plant from time to time, particularly if you can wander around behind the garden centre and perhaps find plants that would be unsuitable for general sale. The very accident that has ruined a plant for the usual buyer may render a tree more interestingly shaped for the purposes of bonsai and it is well worth keeping an eye open for these possibilities.

Collecting is the second and, incidentally, the oldest method of obtaining bonsai. Trees found in the wild were the first to be used for bonsai. Affected by conditions of weather and environment they were often stunted and twisted and very picturesque in shape. These were taken up with the utmost care and with a ritual of an almost religious nature. Sometimes it took several years to remove a chosen tree as the roots on one side would be severed first and the soil replaced, the following year the remainder of the roots would be separated and again the soil would be replaced.

15   *Gathering from the wild.*

By this method the tree, if an old specimen, would not receive such a severe shock and would be easier to re-establish on the final lifting and potting up because the root system would be reasonably compact and ready for transferring to a container.

The Japanese are very skilled at lifting trees of considerable age and, of course, these are already shaped by natural conditions and require maintaining in their natural form rather than 'making' into a bonsai. It is possible to practise this method of lifting trees

29

if a suitable subject is found. It may be necessary to obtain permission if the plant is anywhere but in one's own garden; there are regulations governing the removal of plants even from common land and it would be as well to discover what these are. Again, if following this method, remember to mark the spot so that it is easy to locate the tree on the next visit. When the taproot is finally cut and the tree, with its new, compact root system, is finally lifted it should be well wrapped to contain the ball of soil and root then kept in fairly moist conditions—a large plastic bag, big enough to contain the whole plant, would be ideal. The best time for this work is in the spring just before growth for the year commences. However, it is possible to lift plants in full leaf if sufficient care is taken to retain as much root as possible. In this case the tree may be planted in the garden and the root pruning may be started when the tree has become established in its new site. This will, of course, take longer but it may not be possible to re-visit the original site if the distance is too great. Any plant lifted in this way, that is in full leaf, should be sprayed frequently to prevent it from losing moisture and should also be shaded for a while until it can become established. The soil should approximate as nearly as possible to that of the site from which the tree was lifted; if the native soil was poor, gradual improvement can be made until the plant is ready to be potted up and the correct loam used.

Collecting bonsai from the wild may appear to be a rather long term business but, on the other hand, the tree is, after only a few years in your possession, a much more mature tree than one grown in the same time from seed or cuttings. It is also valuable to collect young seedling trees in the wild but these will have a much smaller root system and will be easier to handle. In this case it is the maturing of the tree that is the long term proposition. A gardener must be a patient man and this applies to an even greater extent in bonsai culture.

There are a few basic points to watch for whether buying a nursery grown plant or collecting from the wild:—

1. The plant should be reasonably small and compact.
2. An attractive appearance is necessary—the disposition of the branches should be balanced and interesting.
3. The trunk should be thick in proportion to the height.
4. The tree should present a reasonably healthy appearance—a sickly tree will be difficult to re-establish, particularly in the hands of a novice.
5. The root system of the tree should also be healthy.
6. Lastly, choose a tree with small leaves or needles and one whose fruit and flowers, if any, will be in proportion to your miniature tree.

Quite a large number of imported trees are available, among them are chinese juniper, maples, elm, crab apple, wisteria and winter jasmine to mention only a few.

From ordinary nurseries I have obtained such plants as cryptomeria japonica, juniper (squamata meyeri), thuya rheingold, picea (spruce) and mugo pines. These have mostly been small plants and no very drastic pruning has been required.

We have, roughly, one acre of garden and I have collected many small trees from it. Pines, beech, oak, chamaecyparis and sorbus, all of which have seeded themselves. Similar trees may be collected in the wild by those with smaller (and tidier) gardens than ours.

The third method of obtaining bonsai is by propagation. Producing one's own plants by growing them from seed, cuttings, division, layering or, more difficult, by grafting. When using these various ways of propagating it will be found that certain trees are grown more easily by one process than another. In theory it is possible to grow any tree from its seed—if you can find it! But in practice some trees are very difficult to grow in this

31

way but relatively easy to cultivate from cuttings or layers. In the chapter on species I shall indicate the best method of propagating the various trees, but a little observation of the habits of trees or a little thought will show that you probably already know the best trees to grow from seed. Anyone living near a sycamore tree, for instance, will have no difficulty in finding seedlings and also in collecting seed and growing his own. Acorns, too, begin to develop as soon as they are ripe and conditions are suitable for growth.

To gather seed of this type at the right time of the year is to ensure success. But seed varies considerably in the time and conditions required for germination, some species taking up to two years to commence growth, and that needs a great deal of patience, even for a bonsai grower. The more fleshy seed, like that of the oak, chestnut and so on, are comparatively easy to grow given the right conditions for germination. They require air, warmth and sufficient moisture.

Moisture is required to soften the outer covering of the seed so that when the root and leaves start to grow they may push through to the soil and air to obtain the necessary nourishment for continuing development. The degree of warmth varies with each species, depending mainly on the temperature of its country of origin. Air is important to the seedling both chemically and biologically, and great care should be taken to give the seedlings sufficient air and light—failure to do so results in poverty-stricken, leggy plants totally unsuited for bonsai culture. Some of the fleshy seeds develop more quickly if soaked in water for a short while but usually it is sufficient to plant them in good loam, a little on the sandy side, and keep them watered, ensuring at the same time that there is sufficient drainage so that the seed does not become waterlogged and rot. Larger tree seedlings will develop a tap root and, therefore, it is best to sow them directly into a fairly shallow container so that there is no need to shock the plant by removing the tap root at a later date in order to fit it in to a suitable container.

Hard coated seeds are more difficult to grow. These usually require stratification, the process used to soften the coat in this instance. The seed should be placed in sand in pans or boxes and left out in the weather for twelve to eighteen months. In this way the frost and other weather conditions help to soften the hard outer coating and prepare the seed for germination. Some hard coated seeds grow readily in the garden. This may be due to the fact that the berries are eaten by birds; the fleshy part of the berry is digested by the bird but the hard coat of the seed is not and is excreted. Although the bird is not able to digest the seed its digestive processes have softened the seed coat and so hastened germination. A hard coated seed may also be nicked with a sharp knife to aid germination.

When the seed, be it hard or soft coated, is ready for sowing, use clean pots or boxes with plenty of drainage. The containers should be well crocked to prevent the soil washing out and really clean so that seedlings are not lost through disease. Use a good compost; drainage is helped by a sandy compost and when the roots begin to develop they don't have to push through heavy, sodden soil. As a general rule a seed needs to be covered with soil to about its own depth and if, initially, the soil is firmed carefully there is no danger of it settling down at a later date and giving

16   *Seed in glass covered shallow pan.*

the seed insufficient protection. Do not sow too many seeds in one pan or box, it will only make difficulties when removing the seedlings, it is so easy to damage the tender young roots.

Leave about half an inch of space at the top of the pan for

watering—this will be necessary when the seedlings start to grow. The best way to water the seed pans is to stand them in a shallow vessel of water which should come to within an inch of the top of the pan. The water will gradually percolate through the soil and when moisture can be seen on the surface the pans may be taken out and drained. A clean sheet of glass or polythene stretched over the top of the pan will keep it from drying out. The pan should not be left unprotected in the sun but should have sufficient light. As soon as the seeds germinate the covering should be removed and the seedlings given enough water and light to develop into healthy young plants. Some seeds will germinate outside without any difficulty, others require a frame outdoors or a warm windowsill. Usually only small numbers of seeds are required for bonsai but it is safer to plant more than you actually need in case some fail to germinate.

A growing number of seed merchants are now advertising seed of trees suitable for bonsai but not all of these are for the novice and many of them can be grown more easily from cuttings or layers. Gathering seed and propagating from it is often satisfactory but do label the pots and give them up to two years before despairing! It is infuriating to turn out barren pots of compost and, later, to find treasured seedlings coming up quite happily on the rubbish dump without all the tender care lavished upon them in the previous months.

The main advantage of raising trees from seed is that for mame or fingertip bonsai you have a really young plant to train. The seed must always be sown in shallow containers in this case and therefore will require more attention to ensure that they do not dry out. If the following experiment is carried out it will show more clearly than words how the growth of seedlings can differ. Take some easily grown seed, possibly sycamore or birch, and sow some in the normal manner and the rest in a shallow container as for mame bonsai. The difference in the rate of growth of the plants will be very marked and the confined root of the seedling in the shallow container will help to reduce the size of the part of the plant which is above the ground.

Many trees and shrubs are easily grown from cuttings and it is, of course, a quicker method of raising stock for bonsai culture. Moreover, when propagating by means of cuttings you are sure of retaining the characteristics of the parent plant. Seed can vary and out of a dozen seedlings there may only be one that is true to the species; with cuttings each one will inherit the nature of the plant from which it is taken. Prunings from other bonsai may be used for cuttings and useful stock grown from a tree which has already proved a satisfactory subject. Having bought a suitable cryptomeria from a nursery I found that the first pruning required the top portion of about one and a half inches to be removed; this was potted as a cutting and is now a small, but thriving, tree.

Occasionally it is necessary to remove a comparatively large branch from a tree to achieve a good shape and it is always worth trying these as cuttings. If they take successfully, and with some species cuttings up to one inch in diameter can be grown with excellent results, a good start, worth several years to the grower, has been made towards another bonsai.

There are various types of cuttings from which it is possible to grow plants, but for our purpose, that of growing shrubs or trees, we need cuttings of soft, half ripe or hard wood. It must be remembered that, when a cutting is to be propagated, a whole plant is to be grown from a portion of the plant that is incomplete. Roots must be made to grow so that the rest of the plant may be nourished. Until the roots develop the top of the plant must nourish itself and also help with the formation of the root system. However, if too much leaf is retained, the cutting loses more moisture than is good for it through transpiration, so some of the

35

leaves and often portions of the remaining leaves must be removed
to lessen this danger. All leaves which will be below ground level
must also be removed.

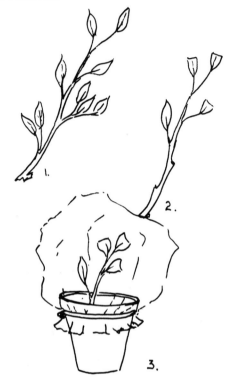

17   *Soft wood cutting.*
1. *As cut.*
2. *Prepared cutting.*
3. *Potted cutting covered with polythene.*

Soft wood cuttings are made from young shoots before the soft,
sappy nature is lost. These are best taken in the spring. The
cutting should be about three inches in length and should be
inserted into the soil for about one third of this length. Cuttings
should be severed from the parent plant immediately below a leaf

Bonsai Juniperus sargentii

Bonsai maple

node so that it may take in water more easily; this is also the most likely point from which the roots will start to grow. It is not always necessary to use a rooting compound but I do—rather on the principle of 'better to be safe than sorry'—and, if the end of the cutting is dipped into water first the powder will adhere more easily. Prepare a pan, box or pot (depending on the number of cuttings) with good, sandy loam. It should be well crocked for good drainage as poorly drained cuttings will rot very quickly. Cuttings may be grown in sand alone but these will have to be watched very carefully because, once the roots are formed, there is no nourishment in the sand to further healthy growth.

Insert the cuttings to the correct depth into firmed soil then water gently with a fine rose; in this way there is no risk of disturbing the cuttings and the remaining leaf is sprayed at the same time. I find it helps considerably to keep the cuttings covered with a polythene bag for a while to retain moisture and cut down the need for constant watering which may waterlog the soil. This is quite easy to do when only small numbers of cuttings are required as is the case when propagating for bonsai.

Eventually the cuttings will show tiny points of new growth or roots will appear at the drainage hole of the pot. Any covering may now be removed and, if more than one cutting is in each pot it would be as well to remove each one to its own pot—the roots soon become entangled and may be damaged if potting on is left too late. A more nourishing soil may now be used and water given regularly. Some cuttings produce new growth before they are rooted so take care when lifting and if no root is visible on the first cutting leave the remainder in place for longer. Others will make a good root system but no top growth for some time—if these are left too long the roots may be damaged when they are separated. I have found that, when I have only one or two cuttings to deal with, a peat pot is useful. The cutting should be prepared

37

and planted in the same way but omitting the crocks in the bottom of the pot. After watering, a polythene bag is placed over the whole of the pot to within about an inch of the base and tied in place. This prevents the pot from drying out too quickly and, if it is placed in a plastic saucer a little water—just as much as it will absorb—may be given from time to time. The cutting may be left in the peat pot until the roots appear through the sides of the pot, at which time the cutting will be well rooted. The polythene covering may be removed as soon as growth is observed but the pot must never be allowed to dry out. When potting on, it is not necessary to remove all the peat and those parts penetrated by the roots may be retained and will help to hold moisture and nourish the new plant.

Half ripe cuttings are taken in the summer and are rather firmer than the soft wood cuttings taken in the spring. Rooting of these will probably take longer and a less sandy soil should be used.

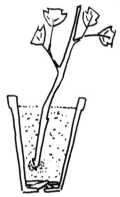

18   *Base of half ripe cutting resting on sand.*

If a small amount of sand is allowed to run into the hole for the base of the cutting to rest on, rooting will be easier—water cannot collect at the base of the shoot and there is no obstruction when the roots commence to develop. Rooting compound can be used and care should be taken that the cutting does not have a space beneath it but rests firmly on the soil or sand at its base. The compost should be firmed around the cutting; watering will help to settle it further but do not firm it after watering or the soil may become too closely packed and delay, or prevent, rooting.

Hard wood cuttings are taken in the early autumn, September or October. They should be of the current year's growth which has hardened. These cuttings should be a little longer than the previous ones and care should be taken that the wood is mature, any cutting which is only half ripe taken at this time will not live until roots can be formed. The preparation of the shoot is similar to that of the half ripe and soft wood cuttings. Hard wood cuttings may remain dormant during the winter but in the spring roots will be produced and new growth will be evident above the

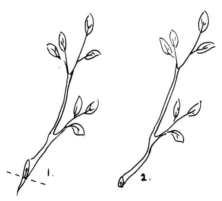

19   *Hard wood cuttings.*
1. *As cut.*
2. *Heel trimmed.*

ground. These cuttings require a less sandy soil than the half ripe or soft wood variety as they are likely to be in it rather longer. Some may be planted in the open ground and take no harm. Sometimes a heel is left on these cuttings when they are prepared but usually a shoot taken immediately below a leaf node will root quite as well as one with a heel. If a heel is left, trim it neatly—a ragged heel is more likely to rot. Again, a little sand at the bottom of the hole made for the cutting is a good idea.

Hard wood cuttings will require less watering because they are grown in cooler weather when the moisture does not evaporate so quickly, but, if they are grown outdoors, keep a watch over them in frosty weather so that if they are raised out of the ground by frost they may be pressed back immediately. Failure to do this will result in loss of cuttings. When roots and buds begin to form in the spring they will need water.

Remember:—

Soft wood cuttings are taken in the spring and root fairly quickly.

Half ripe cuttings are taken in the summer and roots develop more slowly.

Hardwood cuttings are taken in the autumn and probably do not root until the following spring.

As with seed it is vital that all the pans should be clean and well drained. As an extra precaution keep your cutting tools clean—some plants are poisonous to others and your cuttings will be doomed before planting.

When the rooted cuttings are ready for re-potting, pot them up singly. This will give each a chance to develop a good root system which is so essential to bonsai culture. A little well-diluted liquid manure may be given after about six months. The cuttings will now be in a richer soil but must not be allowed to dry out. Plenty of light and air are also required for firm, healthy growth.

Among my own bonsai are a variety grown from cuttings; these include acers, wisteria, lilac, chamaecyparis and many others. Pruning the top of a cryptomeria gave me a well rooted cutting in nine months.

Layering is one of the best methods of obtaining bonsai. Unlike the cutting, the layer is maintained and aided in root production by the parent plant. In many cases, branches of shrubs, or even trees, will layer themselves without any help from Man, so this is really a more natural form of propagation than the taking of cuttings. There are two methods of layering; the one, where a branch or shoot is bent down to the ground and the other, Chinese or air layering. Both are equally suited to our purpose and a fine bonsai can be chosen and rooted by this method. Air layering has a secondary use in the culture of bonsai in that it can be a convenient way of shortening the trunk of a tree that has grown too 'leggy'. A new set of roots can be produced on the trunk where required and, when these have become well established, the trunk may be cut away below this point and potted up in the usual way.

The first mentioned method of layering is very simple and it is carried out if the branch to be rooted will bend sufficiently to reach the ground. Selection of the layer is important when the branch is to be formed into a bonsai and all the principles of a good bonsai should be borne in mind. Try to picture the branch as it will be when severed from the parent plant and potted up. Having chosen the branch to be used a little preparation of the soil beneath will help with the rooting. Fork it well and add a little sand and peat to lighten it if this appears necessary, the layer, like the cutting, must be encouraged to form a good, fibrous root system as soon as possible. The branch is prepared by cutting a shallow notch at the point where the roots are required, or a simple slit may be made and held open by a small pebble. At this point the branch must be 'planted' into the prepared earth and firmed into place. It will probably be necessary to peg this section down with a wooden peg and the top, which is to be the new plant, may need a stake, particularly when an upright form of bonsai is contemplated. The layer should not be

41

severed from the parent plant until it has a good root system and should, even after separating, be left in place for a while to produce sound roots. This process is successful with most plants if carried out between spring and autumn and the layers are

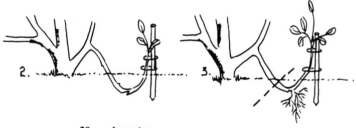

20   *Layering.*
     1. *Selected branch.*
     2. *Prepared layer planted.*
     3. *Severance point of rooted layer.*

usually sufficiently well rooted to be severed in the following spring and potted up in the autumn, by which time the root system should be well formed. Some plants may take two years to layer successfully, this being the case when layering azaleas and other hard wood shrubs. Soft wood layers root relatively easily and should produce roots in six to eight weeks.

Air layering is a very old method of propagating and is said to have been used by the Chinese, hence the name, from whom we learnt the art over two centuries ago. If the portion of the branch required is too high to reach the ground then it must be rooted

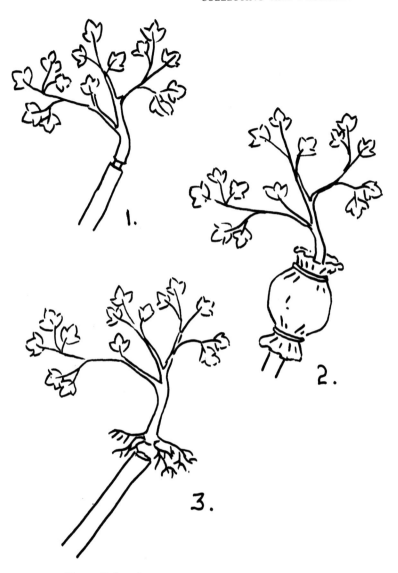

21 *Air layering.*
  1. *Prepared branch.*
  2. *Wrapped in compost and moss and vinyl covered.*
  3. *Rooted layer severed.*

where it is. Once again, choose carefully the part of the branch to be used and visualise the tree that it will be. Having selected the branch, cut a ring of bark about half an inch wide out of it. The thickness of this ring will need to be varied with the branch selected. Generally speaking, the larger the branch the wider and deeper the ring of bark to be removed. If the branch is not very sturdy let the ring be incomplete so that a small portion of the bark is left untouched. The Japanese method of ringing the bark is to use copper wire; the wire is fastened round the tree and

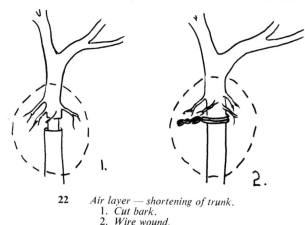

22　　*Air layer — shortening of trunk.*
　　　1. *Cut bark.*
　　　2. *Wire wound.*

tightened sufficiently to bite into the bark. The flow of sap is hindered and the section of the branch above the wire is compelled to produce roots in order to survive. The prepared part of the branch may now be dusted with hormone powder (as for cuttings) and, either wrapped around with damp sphagnum moss and polythene, or a halved flower pot may be clamped around the branch and filled with a suitable compost. Great care must be taken to ensure that the moss or compost is kept sufficiently moist to encourage the growth of the new roots. Do not attempt this type of layering until all risk of frost is over; warm, humid weather is best for this operation and if the weather becomes hot and dry, water as necessary. When the roots have developed cut the tree off below the rooted portion, remove the pot or polythene carefully to avoid damaging the tender roots and pot up in a flower pot until a really good root system is established. The bonsai may then be potted up in a suitable container.

Layering is rather a long term business, but when the bonsai grown by this method is finally potted up it is a fine, mature tree that would have taken many more years to grow from seed or even from a cutting. I have successfully layered and used as bonsai species such as wisteria, hydrangea petiolaris, winter jasmine, azalea, rhododendron and many others.

Another relatively simple method of propagation is by division. Although simple in itself it is suitable only for certain species of plants but, as with layering, the plant propagated in this way will have the same characteristics as the parent stock. Any plant which throws up suckers from the roots around its base will be suitable for this form of propagation. Unless the suckers are coming from a stock onto which the scion of another of the species has been grafted, the new plant will have all the features of the parent. If the original plant has been grafted onto a common stock, as maybe in the case of an ornamental cherry, then the sucker will have the characteristics of the stock plant—probably a wild cherry.

The sucker should be taken from the parent plant in spring or autumn, spring is usually the best time as new growth is imminent and a good root system will be established the sooner. Uncover the sucker and sever it from the parent plant with a sharp knife. It is a good idea to dust both the cut edges with hormone powder or possibly with sulphur to guard against decay. Trim off any damaged or weak roots and any unwanted woody roots; the remaining plant should be strong and healthy and will require potting up in the usual way.

45

In my own collection of bonsai I have several grown from suckers. Lilac, robinia and wild cherry—from the stock of an ornamental cherry—have all been successfully propagated and are now taking shape as bonsai. A favourite plant for bonsai in Japan is bamboo which may be easily propagated by division.

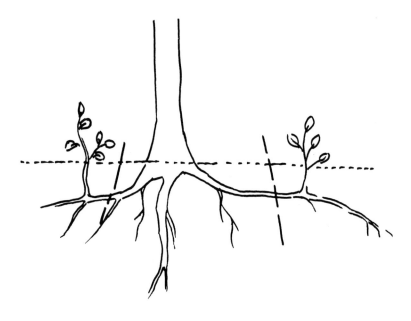

23   *Division showing severance points.*

Grafting is used both for propagating bonsai and for improving an existing tree. Most gardeners will be familiar with the principles of grafting, at the very least, and will realise that many flowering and fruiting plants are made up from two plants. The vigorous root stock, which will furnish the root system for the new plant, is usually a common variety; the scion, supplying branches and shoots, is an ornamental variety of the common stock. For example, a named variety of crab apple will be grafted onto a root stock of a wild crab apple. It is most important that the stock and the scion of the proposed tree should be closely allied to each other.

When cutting straight across the trunk or branch of a tree you will see, between the bark and the wood, a thin layer of green. This is called the 'cambium layer' and is composed of cells which are capable of uniting with other cells of a similar type so that the two may grow together. Whichever form of grafting is used it is important that the cambium layer of the stock must be joined to the cambium layer of the scion.

Although it is possible to grow a well developed bonsai in a relatively short time by grafting, it is a form of propagation that will require practice. It may be possible to produce a successfully grafted tree fairly quickly but more skill is needed to produce a grafted tree on which the join of the stock and the scion is not an unsightly swollen scar. The Japanese are very expert at this process and many trees are propagated by this method in their nurseries.

There are a number of different grafting processes for different purposes but of these only two are generally used for bonsai, the top graft and the side graft. Spring is considered the best time for grafting, early spring for evergreens and a little later for deciduous trees. It is also possible to graft evergreens in early autumn—say the last two weeks of August and the first two weeks of September, but the rising sap of the spring helps to bind the scion and the stock together and loss through a hard winter is less likely.

For a top graft select a suitable stock and scion and, with a sharp knife, cut the scion to a length of two or three inches and, where it is to be united to the stock, cut it at an angle. Cut the selected stock straight across at the point where the graft is to be made—if the join is made low there is a chance of hiding an ugly scar—and make a slit on one side of the top of the stock to match

47

the depth of the angled cut of the scion. Put the scion into the slit of the stock with the angled cut towards the centre of the stock.

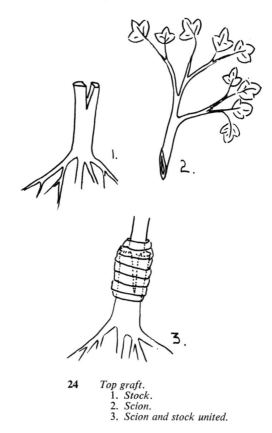

24 *Top graft.*
  1. Stock.
  2. Scion.
  3. Scion and stock united.

Work as quickly as possible so that the sap may unite the two. Bind the join with wide raffia or strips of polythene and plant the whole in a pot as if potting on a cutting. The two plants should be growing as one in about a year.

Where the side graft is used the scion is prepared in the same way but the stock of the plant is left intact. The scion is cut at an angle as before and a slanting cut matching it is made in the trunk of the stock at the desired spot. The scion and the stock are placed together, the angled face of the scion to the inner surface of the slit in the stock. The graft is bound and the whole repotted.

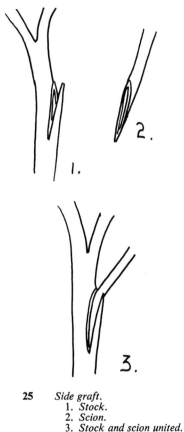

25   *Side graft.*
      1. *Stock.*
      2. *Scion.*
      3. *Stock and scion united.*

If the scion is thriving after about twelve months, the binding may be removed and the top of the stock above the graft may be cut away.

The side graft can also be used to improve the shape of a tree. Where a length of trunk would be enhanced by the addition of a branch, a careful side graft could produce the necessary balance. It is always essential to use closely allied stock and scion for

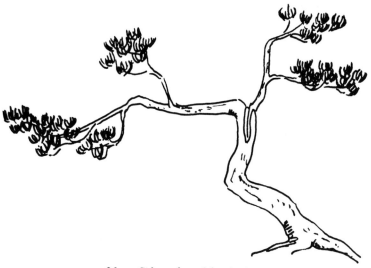

26   *Side graft used for shaping.*

grafting and where a branch is being added for shaping the same rule applies. The new branch must be the same as its fellows or there may be a difference in growth rate and the harmony of the tree will be spoiled.

I think of all methods of propagation this one needs the greatest degree of neatness and dexterity. An ugly graft could spoil a tree but a neatly executed join will produce a fine bonsai within a few years.

4

Care and Maintenance

It is still a widely held belief that a bonsai results from the starving and maiming of a tree. To some extent this is brought about by the appearance of some of the much-wired trees that are imported into this country. Tortured they certainly look, and many have been left far too long in the wire so that it is difficult to remove. Some of the fine trees that are to be found in the gardens of the larger importers or in the all too infrequent exhibitions defy description. We would find no pleasure in these trees if they were not things of beauty, and a tree that is not healthy cannot be beautiful. The tree is planted in a small container and it should receive unremitting care. Some attention is imperative every day; even if there is nothing to be done but the daily watering the plants will benefit from regular observation.

Young trees require more care than the very old ones. They grow at a faster rate and, if allowed to get out of hand, will soon be bonsai no longer. Trees in the wild that are five years old grow at a prodigious speed but when the tree is fifty years old the rate has slowed considerably and is no longer clearly discernible.

The various methods of obtaining bonsai have been described in the previous chapter and each of these requires a different technique when potting up.

ROOT WRAPPED TREES

These are obtainable from late autumn through to the spring; at this time of year the plant is dormant and time spent out of the soil will do little harm. It is always best to go and choose your tree but if a tree is selected from a catalogue of a reliable dealer, the tree is sure to have been packed so that it arrives in good condition. Careful packaging is essential to avoid damaging the shoots of the tree as, in some cases, the loss of the dormant buds will mean the loss of leaves and, more important, the loss of shoots that may spoil the future shape of the tree.

Before unwrapping the root all the requirements should be to hand—soil, pot, water and tools—so that once started the potting up process may proceed uninterrupted. The tree should be studied with an eye to its shape and size. A root-wrapped tree will have had some training so you will simply need to decide on the shape and size of the container and the style to which the tree, in its present form, is most suited. Several grades of soil should be to hand—a coarse, gravelly soil for the bottom of the container which will help with drainage, then a good potting compost to which may be added, depending on the tree, sand, peat or leaf mould in varying amounts. The importance of good drainage is paramount; besides water the roots must have air and both must have free passage. The well mixed soil should have coarse as well as fine particles, good loam and leaf mould for nourishment and some water retentive soil so that it will not dry out too quickly.

When the pot is chosen and prepared, with a crock or plastic mesh over the drainage hole, the roots of the tree may be unwrapped and gently separated. As the tree will have received some training there will be little or no root pruning needed and potting up can proceed. The first layer of soil should consist of a coarse gravel or the sieved out, larger lumps of the compost.

27   *Pot, soil and plant.*

A layer of finer material comes next and the tree is placed in position on this. More of the finer material is added gradually. Work the soil carefully round the roots, a gentle tap on the side of the container will help to settle the soil, and finish the firmed surface with pebbles or moss depending on the appearance required. There should be a space of about half an inch between this top layer and the edge of the container to allow room for watering. Potting should be carried out with a fairly dry soil, so when this is finished, water at once. Place the tree out of the wind and sun and water thoroughly but gently. If preferred the container can stand in a vessel of water, the surface of the water coming about two thirds of the way up the container; when the moisture shows on the surface of the soil, lift out the container and leave it to drain, spray the top of the tree. When the plant has received sufficient water it will drain from the hole in the base of the container; watering must continue until this happens. The tree should be sprayed from time to time but water will not be required in great quantities until the roots start to grow again.

SEED AND CUTTINGS

Plants grown from seed and cuttings need to be grown on in ordinary pots or in the open ground for a couple of years before they are ready to pot as bonsai. Some training of the top of the tree can be carried out if it is necessary but the trunk and root system need this time to develop. When the tree is taken up for potting the roots must be trimmed to produce a more compact root system and, in particular, any tap root must be shortened to fit into the container. Apart from this the young plant requires the same treatment as a root wrapped tree.

If the seed or cuttings have been grown in peat pots some of the outer roots will have penetrated the peat. Do not attempt to remove the pot. Break away the rim and as much of the rest as may be free of roots and plant the remainder in the container. The tree will grow on with hardly any setback at all and the presence of the peat will be beneficial rather than harmful.

COLLECTING FROM THE WILD

The potting treatment of these trees depends to some extent on the circumstances. A small tree—a second year seedling for instance—may be treated as a cutting or seedling grown at home. The larger specimens require more expert handling. In the section on collecting trees I have outlined the method of lifting a tree over a couple of years. With the larger trees this is a good idea if it can be carried out successfully. However it may not be possible, due to the distance and time involved, and in that case more care must be taken, when lifting the tree, to take it up with as large a root ball as possible. Watering before lifting will help to keep the ball of soil together and is particularly necessary if the weather has been dry. Lift the tree on to sacking or polythene sheeting, wrap the roots securely and tie so that the root ball is covered and all the moisture will be retained. If the tree is in leaf (not the best time to lift it, but it may be unavoidable) spray the foliage thoroughly to prevent loss of moisture. The tree should be planted in the ground or in a large flower pot which will contain the whole

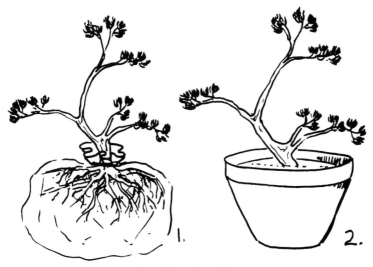

28   *Collected from the wild.*
   1. Lifted and wrapped in polythene.
   2. Initially planted in large pot.

root ball. After a couple of months, when the tree has had time to recover, the shaping and training of the plant may begin. The following year it should be possible to lift the tree and trim the roots ready for potting. If the root ball was very large it would be advisable to return the tree to the pot or to the garden for another year after trimming until the fine root system that is required begins to develop. When the tree is ready to put into the chosen container, a final trimming of the roots will be necessary and then the potting up may follow the procedure as for a root wrapped tree.

A nursery bed that may be used for growing on cuttings, seedlings and trees from the wild is useful. Trees that need to have the trunk thickened may spend a year or two in such a bed. Bonsai training may continue and the tree can be lifted periodically to keep the roots in check, but the trunk will increase in girth much more rapidly than if left in the container. Any wiring on the tree needs watching if this is done so that the wire is not allowed to bite into the bark. Loosen the wire from time to time to prevent this. The bed may also be used for a tree that is not thriving. Six months or a year will usually suffice to improve the condition of a poor looking tree.

NURSERY GROWN TREES

In this country a fair number of our trees will be nursery grown. Some nurseries are now growing stock which they recommend for bonsai but even from others it may be possible to obtain suitable specimens. To buy a nursery grown tree for bonsai it is necessary to shop personally. So much depends on the shape of the tree, thickness of the trunk and other factors. Most nursery plants are now offered for sale all the year round and to enable the nursery to do this the plants are potted up in plastic or disposable cardboard pots at the right time of the year and then they may be removed from the nursery for 'instant gardening' at any time, without waiting for the dormant season. This system is of great advantage to the bonsai grower for, to some extent, the root system is already reasonably compact.

The tree may be left in the temporary pot until the correct time for potting up, remembering to keep it watered meanwhile. On removing the tree from the pot examine the condition of the root ball. If the pot is full of roots it is as well to wash off the soil that remains to see clearly what needs to be done. Long roots growing round the inside of the pot should be trimmed by about two thirds. The tap root should be cut by the same amount if it is in evidence, making sure that the cut is diagonal to prevent the cut end rotting.

It is usually necessary to reduce the mass of roots considerably when the tree has been grown for the purpose of planting in the garden. To make a bonsai the tree requires a good root system but it needs to be much more compact and to have more fine feeding roots near the base of the trunk than a garden plant. If the mass of roots is very large, pruning may be done gradually in two or three stages, each time planting the tree in a smaller pot until it becomes possible to use a correctly proportioned bonsai container. While the root ball is being reduced a certain amount of trimming will probably be required for the branches. This may be carried out in proportion to the amount of root that is removed. A reduced root system should not be expected to support the same amount of foliage and so this may be proportionately reduced— always bearing in mind the style of bonsai towards which you are aiming. If the correct potting up procedure is used (as described in the treatment of root wrapped trees) each time the tree is repotted, a compact, fine-rooted system will be developed by the time the tree is ready for its final planting in a bonsai container.

LAYERS, GRAFTS AND DIVISIONS

Trees propagated by these methods may be treated in the same way as cuttings. Growing on for a while in a nursery bed or a large pot is most helpful for thickening the trunk and developing the root system but after this period has passed potting up will follow the accepted method.

REPOTTING

If the matter is urgent and sufficient care is used, repotting may be carried out at almost any time. However, I would stress that this is for the more experienced grower and the novice would do well to keep fairly closely to the seasons recommended for each species. By and large it is safe to follow the rules accepted by any gardener. A tree is best moved in its dormant season. A spring flowering tree should be moved in the autumn, deciduous trees may be moved in autumn or early spring and conifers generally may be moved at any season but mid-summer and mid-winter. A bonsai is often a hardy tree and will remain outdoors the year round. There are exceptions to this and half hardy or delicate trees should winter under cover. However, when deciding on the correct time for repotting it is best to work on the premise that the tree will be outside the year round and to avoid the risk of frost. The most suitable time for repotting, of course, will be just before the tree begins its growth cycle for the year so that the developing roots may take the place of those removed with as little delay as possible.

Let us next examine the reasons for repotting. A bonsai is a 'tree in a tray', a tree in a very small container. To maintain its healthy growth it must be fed and watered. As the tree develops the leaves and branches are trimmed to shape the tree but the root system proceeds to grow. If this is allowed to continue without repotting the container will become far too crowded with roots of the wrong sort; all the nourishment in the soil will have been used, water will drain straight through and will not penetrate the small amount of soil remaining and it is possible that the roots will begin to rot or dry out and die back.

The bonsai grower will observe the condition of his plants each day and will come to know, by experience, when repotting is necessary. Generally speaking young trees require repotting more

xi This Thuya is approximately 8 years old.

xii Removing the Thuya from the container for repotting.

xiii The roots are gently teased out and trimmed.

xiv Watering thoroughly before repotting.

frequently than the older ones as they will be making more growth. Flowering and fruiting trees also require more frequent repotting than other deciduous trees while conifers may be left several years without disturbance. It is helpful, when considering the necessity for repotting, to look at the habits of the tree, its rate of growth—particularly of the roots—and to examine from time to time the drainage hole in the base of the container. A healthy tree will usually have one or two roots showing at the drainage hole but if the number is greater the pot is becoming too crowded for health, (a complete absence of roots at the drainage hole some time after repotting could indicate lack of healthy root development which needs investigating).

Work should, if possible be carried out sheltered from sun and wind to prevent the roots drying out while repotting proceeds. When planning to repot a bonsai allow the soil to become a little dryer than usual so that it may be removed without causing damage and the roots separated more easily. A piece of half-inch dowelling cut straight across is useful to loosen the tree in the container, it can be pushed into the drainage hole and the flat, cut surface will do no harm. Do not lift the tree out before you are sure that the tree is loose or you may tear the roots. If the tree is to be replaced in the same container, which is usually the case, wash the container thoroughly.

A small tree may be held in the hand to loosen the outside layer of soil and roots. A large plant is more difficult to handle and a turntable is useful to rest it upon. The tree may be steadied and turned with one hand while the other removes the soil. You will accumulate your own set of tools for these jobs; in this particular operation something like an old fashioned wooden meat skewer is useful—the Japanese use a chop-stick. Remove the soil from around the sides of the root ball and also from beneath it. Trim the roots as necessary; any over-vigorous or injured roots

61

should be cut off and the general root ball reduced by about two thirds. This will leave plenty of room for fresh soil to be used in the container.

Prepare the pot by covering the drainage holes with nylon mesh or a piece of pot—the mesh takes less room in a small container —to prevent the compost being washed out.

A large tree may need to be fastened into the container and to do this a vinyl covered wire can be threaded up through the holes of the container as illustrated. Coarse gravel or the larger lumps of soil, sieved out of the compost, are placed in the bottom of the container and a layer of finer soil covers this. The depth of this layer depends on the volume of roots to be fitted in. When preparing the compost sieve out and discard the very finest soil as this will tend to settle too closely round the roots and waterlog the container. The more granular compost will allow both the water and air access to the roots.

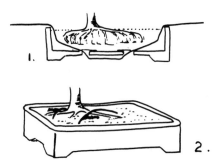

29   *Fastening tree into container.*
      1. *In section.*
      2. *Wires in use.*

Try the tree in the pot, if it needs to be lower remove a little of the top layer of soil; if you want the tree higher in the container —possibly to expose the roots—add a little more soil beneath it.

When the tree is satisfactorily positioned it may be fastened down with the wires, this will hold it firm and prevent any movement of the tree after repotting. Continue to fill the container with soil which should come to within half an inch of the top of the container. The soil should be firmed around the roots, tap the pot gently all round to help the compost to settle. When the soil is nearly up to the half inch level the final layer, which may consist of small stones, moss or tiny ground cover plants, can be added. Take care not to fill the container above this level because sufficient space must be left for watering.

The soil used for repotting should be fairly dry as it retains its porosity better in this state, wet compost pressed around the roots of the tree would tend to exclude the air they need. Once repotting is complete the tree should be watered without delay, it should be placed in the shade, out of the wind and watered with a fine spray. This will enable the soil to absorb the water and the surface will not be displaced as it might with a stronger flow. Watering should continue until the excess runs from the drainage hole showing that the soil is sufficiently saturated. Protection from the sun and wind must be afforded to the tree for the next few weeks. New roots will start to grow in the course of the next six weeks or so and when these are firmly established any wires holding the tree in the container may be cut and removed. Watering should be regulated—the roots must be kept moist but not saturated—after the initial watering which follows repotting. The leaves may be sprayed to prevent loss of moisture but heavy or continuous rain could be injurious at this time. The appearance of new young shoots will indicate successful repotting.

I will deal with the potting up of groups of trees and ishitzuki (clasped-to-stone) towards the end of this chapter.

63

ROOT PRUNING

During the process of repotting one is faced with the task of root pruning. This is carried out for several reasons but not, as many people think, for the purpose of dwarfing the tree. Obviously the small containers will not permit a large root system but pruning the roots promotes the growth of a finer, more compact root system rather than lessening the amount of moisture and nourishment received by the tree. The roots and foliage of the tree depend one upon the other, weak foliage will enfeeble the root system while an over foliated tree will not be fed correctly by the roots. The pruning of roots is a process known to any gardener, not only the grower of bonsai; its aim is to promote healthy

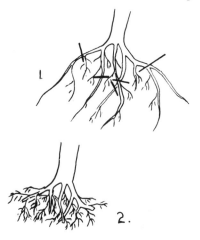

30   Root pruning.
      1. Root and where to prune.
      2. New growth after pruning.

growth, to give a tree a good shape and to increase its flowering and fruiting potential. So we see that while root pruning is necessary for bonsai it does not, in itself, dwarf the tree. Rather, does it help to keep the dwarf tree healthy.

The roots of a tree are divided into two main categories; the fine roots which feed the tree and the larger roots (like the tap root) which help to stabilise the tree. In the culture of bonsai we wish to produce a healthy crop of fine roots to feed the plant but the larger roots which stabilise a naturally grown plant are less important.

Root pruning varies according to the age of the tree. The young, vigorous tree will grow at a greater rate than the mature tree and the roots, therefore, will require closer attention. The tap root must be removed before the tree can be planted in a container, all the longer and coarser roots should be cut back to encourage and make room for the finer fibrous roots. Any broken or dead roots should be trimmed off and when the plant is ready to repot there should be a space of three quarters to one inch between the root ball and the sides of the container. This is filled with fresh soil to nourish the fibrous roots and, through them, the branches and leaves. While the tree is young the large roots should be removed gradually so that a compact system of fine roots is produced by the time the tree is mature. With the older tree repotting does not usually take place so frequently and the roots require trimming to fit the container, rather than pruning. The tree will, when mature, have the type of root system required for healthy growth and will mainly need a little attention to keep the root ball small enough for its container and also to trim out older roots. Always remember that the roots of a tree need air, as well as water and nourishment, so a container overcrowded with roots, or roots packed with heavy airless soil will, in time, damage the tree. Tools used for root pruning should be sharp, to prevent bruising and subsequent rotting of the cut ends, and should be cleaned before moving to the next plant. The juice of some plants is poisonous to others so the neglect of cleaning the cutting tools could harm a treasured tree.

PRUNING

A bonsai is both dwarfed and shaped by pruning. Both operations take place gradually over a number of years and require constant care and attention. The grower aims at a healthy, well proportioned tree with close, fine foliage. The trunk should taper from a wide base to a fine tip with no ugly stumps to show where the tree has been heavily pruned in a clumsy attempt at dwarfing. When the tree is planted in a large pot or nursery bed the pruning of the branches should not be neglected.

If you have obtained an imported tree, the training and pruning for the basic shape will already have been carried out. Your task is to maintain and enhance the style of the tree. This tree will require trimming rather than pruning and a knowledge of how to trim the various species is important.

EVERGREEN

Pines, with the exception of the five needled pine for which such treatment may prove damaging in the following year, should have the sprouts nipped when they are an inch or so long. The sprouts on the lower branches should be removed first, as these are the weaker ones, and new growth will thus be encouraged on the lower branches to keep the balance and shape of the tree. A little later the upper sprouts are removed and numerous new, short-needled sprouts will take their place in the following year. This should not be carried out more than once every three years but it will help to keep the foliage close and short-needled. The other years the 'candles' of the pines may be trimmed (with the fingers) just as the needles begin to show, if they are trimmed by half of their length a reasonable amount of foliage will be produced. This trimming should always be done with the fingers; in the first place the shoot is too far advanced if it cannot be nipped by the fingers and secondly, if scissors or secateurs are used there is a

66

greater danger of cutting the needles. The closer foliage of the five-needled pines will not need a great deal of pinching but should have any shoots removed which threaten to spoil the shape of the tree.

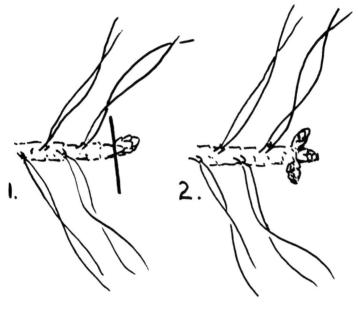

31   *Pruning new growth.*
         1. Removal of sprout.
         2. New growth.

Spruce should be pinched systematically. The buds take some time to open and, starting with the largest, pinching will probably be continued for three weeks or so before the whole tree is trimmed. Pinching should begin when the sprouts are about half developed and it is easy to nip them with the fingers. The greatest care must be taken to pull off only the part of the shoot not required, the needles are so fine that they may be easily damaged. A spruce bonsai that has been established for some years may

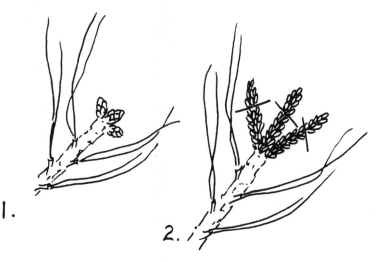

32 *Trimming of new growth.*
   1. Sprouts.
   2. Removal of half of 'candle'.

33 *Removal of sprouts on:*
   1. Spruce.
   2. Juniperus Chinensis.

Juniperus sargentii bonsai

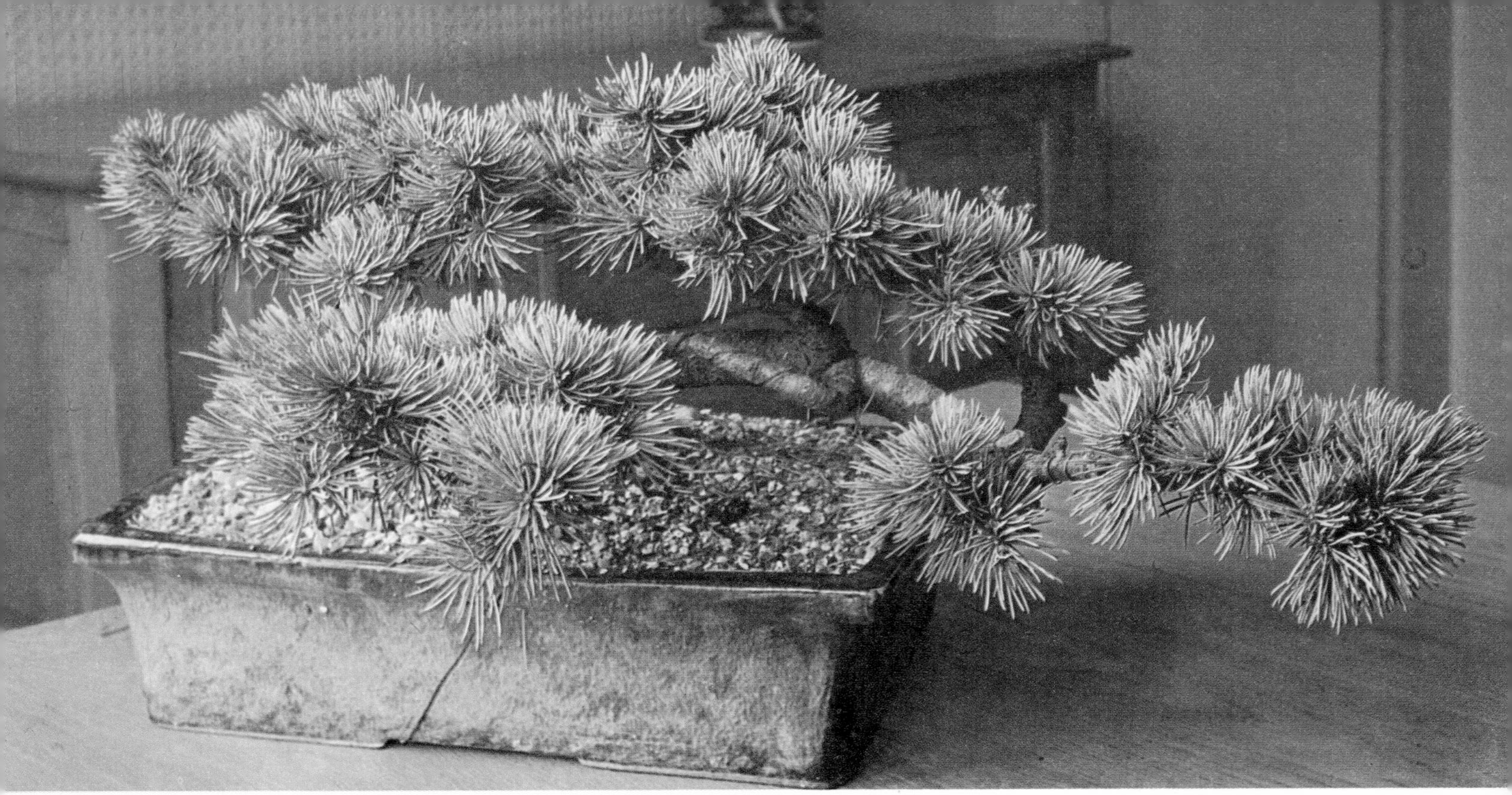

Picea pungens kosteriana (bonsai)

require a severe pinching for one season to tidy up the growth and ensure a shorter needled growth in the following season. This treatment is rather drastic and should only be practised on strong trees and only once in a three year period.

Some evergreens produce new shoots throughout the growing season. Cryptomeria and juniper are cases in point and tips can be removed almost daily. Care must be taken not to cut any portion of the remaining needles as the damaged needles left on the tree will become an unsightly brown. As with spruce the pinching is much better done with the fingers.

Heavy pruning, by which I mean the removal of all or part of a branch, may take place during the warmer part of the year but winter must be avoided. A reasonable time must elapse after repotting to allow the roots to become re-established before any heavy pruning is attempted. An exception to this will have to be made if the tree is recently gathered from the wild and much of the root has been removed—the remaining root may not be capable of supporting the tree as it stands so some basic training of the tree may take place. Heavy pruning will also be necessary to shape a nursery grown tree but in this case the pruning may be carried out while the tree is still in its temporary pot and then, after the tree has recovered from pruning, the reduction of the root mass may begin.

The basic shaping of a bonsai should not be undertaken in a hurry. Consider the tree from all aspects before making any attempt to remove a branch. Decide first the style most suitable for the species with particular attention to the tree as it stands. Be clear in your mind as to which is to be the front and which the back of the tree. At this stage a rough drawing (never mind how amateurish) would probably clarify the situation and help to decide which branches must be removed. Where the natural growth of a tree is symetrical it will present a more pleasing appearance if only one branch is left at each branching point. The first branch should be to the right and the second to the left and so on. Branches jutting out to the front should be removed but one that extends towards the back will help to give the plant a more natural depth. The line of the trunk is very important and should be unbroken for the greater part of its length.

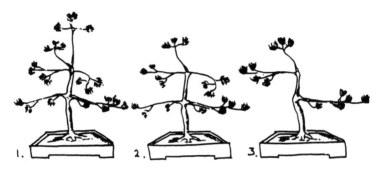

34 *Shaping by pruning.*
   1. Tree to be shaped.
   2. Reduced height.
   3. Finished shaping.

Probably the finest aid to shaping a tree will be found in studying as many pictures of mature bonsai as you can find. No explanation is as good a guide as a pictorial one. Exhibitions of bonsai are very helpful and displays shown by some of the larger importers will repay close observation. Always bear in mind the natural beauty of the tree, its balance and harmony.

DECIDUOUS AND FLOWERING TREES

Deciduous and flowering trees require rather different treatment from that accorded to the evergreens. These trees lose their leaves during the winter and for part of the year they are bare of foliage. The form of the tree is then all important. Those that produce flowers and fruit need special care so that the following years' flower buds are not removed during trimming and the decorative fruits are borne in due season.

As with the evergreen trees the imported varieties are already shaped as bonsai and preservation of the form is what is required. Shoots left to grow too thick and long on a deciduous tree, and then pruned, will result in a clumsy 'snag'. This is sometimes necessary if a lower branch is left in order to thicken the trunk of the tree; where this has been done a Japanese grower would probably turn it to good account, shape the snag, peel the bark away and so produce an old, weatherbeaten appearance. If this does not suit the style of tree it should simply be cut off as closely as possible to the bole when it has performed the task of thickening the trunk.

With deciduous trees the aim should be a thick, aged trunk with young branches and shoots capable of bearing flowers and fruit. The correct potting procedure will help to keep the branches

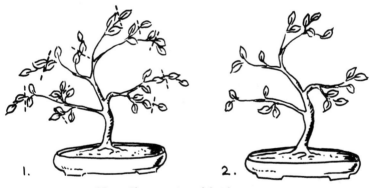

35   *Shoot pruning of deciduous tree.*
       1. Beech in leaf.
       2. Trimmed to one or two nodes.

and shoots young and vigorous but the growth must be checked to preserve the shape and stature of the bonsai and to encourage flowering. As the shoots begin to lengthen and the leaves to

71

appear, they should be nipped back (with the fingers) to about the first or second node, depending on the shape of the tree. Once the shoot has been trimmed to this length, any new shoots appearing at this point should be removed immediately. A vigorous tree will need constant attention during the growing season. Some deciduous trees, the beech for instance, will need trimming only once during the year, while others will produce new shoots throughout the growing season. If it has been necessary to prune the roots or branches of a tree drastically when transplanting, bear this in mind and wait until the tree has become re-established before carrying out the trimming process. The health of the tree is of prime importance if it is to make a good bonsai.

Leaf cutting is practised to reduce the size of the leaves of some trees. Make sure that the tree is vigorous and then, in early summer when the foliage has appeared, cut off the first crop of leaves—just removing the leaf and leaving its stem. The stem will fall shortly and a new crop of smaller, more brilliantly coloured leaves will be produced. Maples, elms and ginkgos all benefit

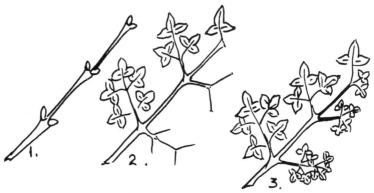

36   *Trimming and leaf cutting of Acer.*
   1. Bare twig.
   2. Right hand side of twig trimmed to two nodes and leaves removed.
   3. Right hand side of twig showing small new leaves.

from leaf cutting; the effect is to give the tree a second autumn and spring in the year with the second crop of leaves being reduced in size. This should never be attempted with trees which have needles rather than leaves.

Flowering and fruiting trees must have these factors taken into consideration when trimming and pruning. As garden fruit trees and flowering shrubs are pruned with regard to the amount of blossom desired, so bonsai which produce flowers and fruit must be trimmed with the same principles in mind. They are pruned depending on the season of flowering and also with attention as to whether the flowers are borne on old or new wood.

A tree which bears flowers on the new wood, as does an azalea or a cherry, may be pruned immediately after flowering. Where the shoots have been removed a number of sprouts will appear. All but one or two of these should be trimmed off and those that remain are cut back to one or two leaves. Flower buds will form later in the season so pinching must not be carried out after this unless it is really necessary. Occasionally it may be worthwhile to sacrifice the following year's flowers by pinching all through the season so that an attractive shape is formed. If the pruning of the shoots is left too late the sprouts that are produced after pruning will not bear flowers.

Where the flower is borne on the old wood, as in the case of the japanese quince, shoots may be left until June and then the tree may be trimmed as required.

Trimming the shoots is an essential part of the dwarfing technique, the new shoots show shorter distances between the nodes and photographic records kept will show how slow the rate of growth becomes over the years. Experience is the best teacher as to which trees require constant trimming through the year and which can be trimmed once to achieve the desired effect.

Heavy pruning of deciduous and flowering trees should be

73

xv A 7 year old Maple in leaf.

xvi Pruning the Maple in the following dormant season.

37   *Japanese Quince.*
      1. Dotted line shows new growth.
      2. Pruned back to old wood.

carried out only when the tree is well established. If the pruning is carried out first, allow the tree time to recover before repotting; or, if the tree has been repotted, allow the roots to commence to grow before pruning. Avoiding the danger of frost (if the tree is kept outside) the dormant period, when growth is not taking place, is the most suitable for heavy pruning. Some species of trees will not tolerate heavy pruning and loss of the tree may result: japanese flowering cherry is a case in point. Again, a vigorously growing tree may react to heavy pruning by producing strong but sappy growth which is quite unsuitable for bonsai and which may well spoil the shape of the tree.

SHAPING BY WIRING

Careful pruning is essential when making a bonsai and many growers try to shape their trees without recourse to wiring. However there are situations where wiring or pressure of some kind is necessary to alter the direction or shape of a branch. I will explain the principles of wiring and also give examples of other methods of forming suitable and pleasing styles.

Wiring is a job for an expert—but experts must start somewhere and I would suggest that branches of a shrub (possibly prunings from the garden) are very useful for practising this art. First perhaps it is necessary to point out the reasons why a tree should be wired.

Formation of style—where a tree does not take the form required naturally. Rather than remove a large part of the trunk of an over tall tree it may be possible to train it into a kengai or

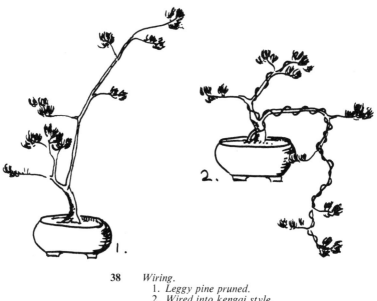

38   *Wiring.*
   1. *Leggy pine pruned.*
   2. *Wired into kengai style.*

cascading bonsai. Or again, the tree may be shortened by wiring and forming into the bankan style where the tree is curved at several points on the trunk. Careful consideration of the tree in question and of the styles available will show how dwarfing and shaping may be carried out without heavy pruning.

Ageing—certain shapes of branches give an appearance of great age. If you study an old tree in the wild the branches will be seen to slope down from the trunk rather than up, the tip of the branch only will turn up. This may be achieved by wiring and the impression of age will be much strengthened.

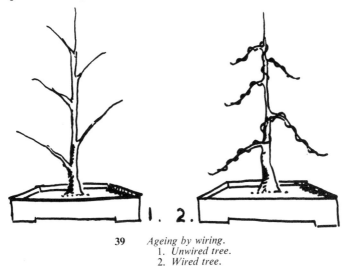

39 *Ageing by wiring.*
  1. *Unwired tree.*
  2. *Wired tree.*

Correction of growth—it may be necessary to alter the position of a branch if it spoils the line of the trunk or cuts across another branch. If the position can be altered by wiring it is preferable to removing the branch and leaving the tree with an unbalanced appearance.

The type of wire used in this process must be firm enough to hold the trunk or branch in position but not so stiff that it will be difficult to bend. Copper wire is usually recommended for the purpose, it is annealed to soften it for use. After heating (annealing) it is cooled and then, when it is in place, it will gradually harden and will hold the branch in position. Wire of varying thicknesses will be needed and discretion must be used as to that which is required for a particular part of the tree, this is where practise comes in useful; it would be very harmful to wire a tree, find the wire too weak and have to re-wire. For very small or

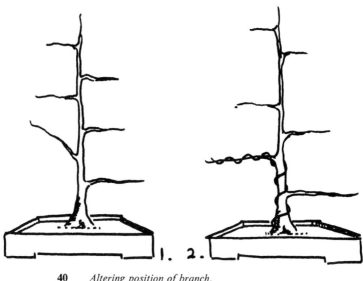

40 *Altering position of branch.*
   1. Unwired tree.
   2. Wired tree with branch positioned correctly.

easily bent shoots I have found varying sizes of vinyl-covered wire very satisfactory and where the delicate bark of a shoot can be injured a pipe cleaner may be the answer. When annealing the wire take care not to heat it so much that it becomes brittle and remember that there are some trees that will not tolerate the copper wire; japanese cherry must be shaped by some other method.

It is difficult to generalise as to which time of the year is the best for this operation. I shall try to indicate the best season for each species in the appropriate chapter but weak trees and those recently repotted should not be wired. The tree will need a little extra care after wiring—shelter from extreme cold and heat would be a sensible precaution. Study the tree carefully before beginning to wire; as with pruning it is better to proceed slowly than to make a mistake. To alter the position of a wired branch after setting may well injure the tissues so badly that it will wither and die. A little extra time spent considering the problem will pay good dividends.

If a tree requires a great deal of wiring it will be as well to do it gradually rather than all at once. For example, wire and shape the trunk first and leave for some months before proceeding with the branches. Wiring the branches at intervals will also minimise the risk of harming the growth.

Where the trunk of the tree is to be wired it is necessary to anchor the end of the wire so that it is stable and will not slip.

41   *Wire secured through drainage hole.*

This can be done while repotting; the wire is threaded through the drainage hole and brought up alongside the plant where it may remain until required. The wire must be coiled very carefully round the trunk; the distance between the coils is governed by the degree of bend required. If a considerable curve is necessary or a very bent trunk is to be straightened the coils should be closer together than if the bends are only slight. Coil the wire closely to the trunk but not so tightly as to injure the bark. The trunk may also be shaped by bending one or two stout pieces of wire into the form desired and binding the trunk to them with

79

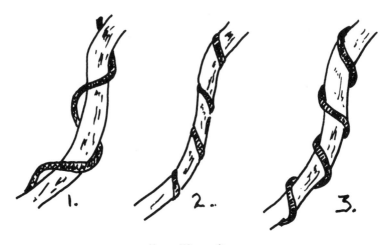

42   *Wire coiling.*
  1. *Too loose.*
  2. *Too tight.*
  3. *Correct.*

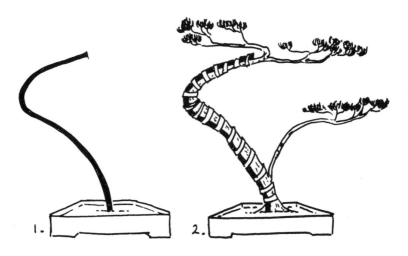

43   *Binding trunk to shaped wire.*

fine wire or raffia. Where the trunk is shaped in this manner the wire may be left in place for a longer period without biting into the bark.

When several branches are to be wired start work on the lower branches. The wire to be used can be fastened under the wire on the trunk or the wire can be coiled once round the trunk first and

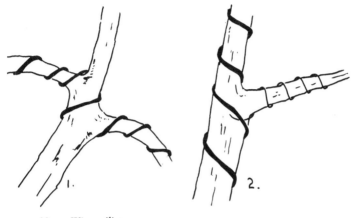

44 *Wire coiling.*
  1. Method for two branches.
  2. Method for one branch using trunk wire as anchor.

the end secured beneath its own loop. Sometimes it is convenient to wire two branches with one wire if they are sufficiently close to one another. Coiling the wire must be carried out with great caution, it may be necessary to protect the branch first if the bark is delicate and care must be taken not to damage leaves or young shoots. Be content to proceed very slowly. When actually bending the wired branch do it gently a little at a time until the required shape is achieved. Time spent practising this delicate operation is of great value. Your hands will need to learn their craft. Sometimes it is better to wire a branch with two fine wires than with one stout one, the shaping is more gentle but equally as efficient.

Allow for a considerable length of wire when coiling—it is fatal to run out of wire before you reach the end of the branch—after a little practice you will be able to estimate the length of wire needed.

A wired tree must be watched. The wire must not be allowed to cut into the bark of the tree. Occasionally wire is left too long on unsold imported trees and the bark begins to grow round it and it is quite impossible to remove. If the wire appears to be getting too tight after about six months loosen it and wire again. This operation may be carried out several times before the tree is finally shaped. The length of time required for setting into shape varies, pines require the longest period of shaping before becoming set. As a rule the larger the diameter of the branch the longer it will take to alter its shape. The new shoot of a wisteria will only

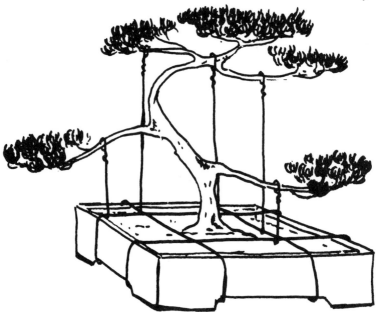

45   *Container wired and branches fastened to wires.*

82

take about six months—by that time the wood will have hardened and the wire may be removed. Never leave a wire in place after it has done its work.

There are several methods of altering the form of trees without resorting to wiring. A reasonably pliant trunk may be shaped by tying the plant down to wires fastened around the container. When the plant is repotted leave it for a while to re-establish itself and develop fresh roots then put your wires in several positions round the container. Pull the trunk gently into the required shape and tie where necessary to the wires. The ties may be shortened gradually to avoid the danger of fracturing the trunk. A cascade or kengai bonsai is often formed in this way. The pot is firmly wired to the display stand (usually necessary with kengai in any case as a gust of wind could overbalance it) and the portion of the trunk to be cascaded is brought down and fastened in the appropriate position. Several months must elapse between the potting up and the start of such shaping.

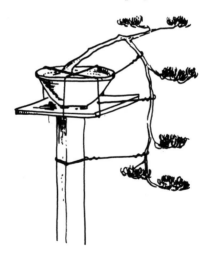

46   *Kengai trained by fastening to wires.*

83

A downward curve may be achieved by hanging a weight on a branch. I was given a very good tip about this—the lead weights used by fishermen can be obtained in various sizes and have either a hole through the centre for cord or wire or a small loop at the top which can be attached to a wire on the branch. This has a great advantage in that the shaping may be carried out gradually and the branch be drawn further down at intervals by merely changing the weight for a heavier one.

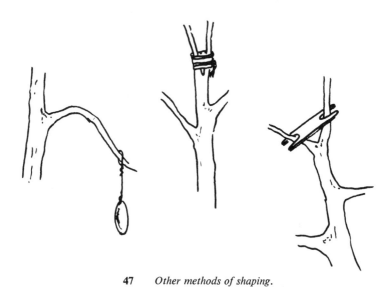

47   *Other methods of shaping.*

Occasionally it is possible to utilise two branches on a tree; they can be tied closer together or a small, shaped wedge—cut from a thin piece of wood, dowelling or bamboo—can be used to prop them apart. If a young, pliable tree requires straightening it may be possible to use a piece of dowelling or bamboo as a splint; the trunk is tied to the splint with raffia or strips of cloth at fairly

Bonsai trees

Bonsai maple (Acer)

close intervals, always taking care not to injure any shoots or small branches.

Remember:—

Do not wire unnecessarily or change your mind once the branch is in position.

Leave time between repotting and wiring for the tree to become established.

Proceed slowly.

Watch carefully so that the wire does not harm the bark of the tree.

Remove the wire as soon as the branch is set.

Cherry trees should not be wired with copper wire.

WATERING, SOIL AND FEEDING

The watering and soil requirements of bonsai are so bound up together that I have dealt with them at the same time. The amount of water given each day must depend, to some extent, on the make-up of the compost. Correct watering of bonsai is of vital importance. Even so, it is mainly a question of common sense. Obviously it is essential that a tree in such a small container must be supplied with sufficient water. How much each tree needs usually depends on the individual species. None of them should ever be allowed to dry out. If the potting compost used is correct and the drainage carefully arranged the soil should never become waterlogged. Bonsai containers have large drainage holes and are raised on legs so that there is no chance of the roots remaining in saturated soil. The compost used must consist of large and small particles, some of the material must be water retentive, and sand must be present to keep it open and porous.

Japanese growers use a nest of sieves varying from a quarter inch to one thirty second of an inch with the finest sieve at the bottom. The soil is passed through these and the finest soil of all is discarded, any other material used—leaf mould, sand etc.—is also sieved and the soils required may be mixed from these graded materials. The coarsest soils are used in the bottom of the container, thus aiding drainage, while the finer grades are filled in round the roots. Some trees will tolerate more water retentive material than others, these are usually trees that require wetter conditions—wisteria, willow and cryptomeria for instance. If your own garden soil is not suitable even with the addition of sand, peat and leaf mould then it is probably wiser to buy a good potting compost and use that. Examine it before buying to be sure that the mixture will do the work that you require.

Watering is carried out almost every day and this is a very good opportunity for observing your plants. Learn to decide which plants need water; by the colour of the soil, weight of the container and lastly by the feel of it—scraping away a little of the top soil with your finger if necessary, a gardener can never expect to keep his hands clean. The correctly potted tree will have a space, varying from a quarter to half an inch between the top of the soil and the edge of the container, for water; pour the water onto the surface of the soil near the bole of the tree until this space is full. It will drain through the soil taking the stale air with it and draw fresh air in to replace the stale. If the compost is unsuitable the water may stand on the surface or, if the tree has been allowed to dry out, it may be difficult for the water to penetrate. Faults in drainage must be corrected for the trees to remain healthy.

During the spring the tree will need sufficient water for new growth. Hot weather will often mean that it is necessary to water twice a day, a reasonable amount twice a day will be better than a soaking in the morning and then allowing the tree to dry out as the day goes on. Shade of some sort will help to prevent the trees drying out too quickly at this time. Watering during the autumn is a matter for observation, give each tree what it needs.

The trees must not be allowed to dry out during the winter but as this is the dormant season they will tend to use less water. Waterlogged soils can turn to ice in hard frost so use your judgement.

Trees with larger leaves—maples and oaks—give off more moisture by transpiration than small leaved trees or those with needles. All trees benefit from spraying from time to time and the larger leaved varieties in particular. Choose your time for spraying, however, it will not do to have water on the leaves during the heat of the day, particularly if the trees are standing in the sun. This would cause the leaves to be scorched as the droplets of water magnify the heat of the rays.

A tree growing in the wild will develop its root system and will absorb what nutriment it requires from the surrounding area. The restricted root of the bonsai must also be able to supply the tree with sufficient nourishment so it becomes necessary to feed with a little fertilizer occasionally. The regular repotting of the trees will ensure sufficient supplies of those elements found in the soil but not required in large quantities. Larger amounts of potassium, nitrogen and phosphoric acid are needed, however, and these may be given by using a fertilizer. A liquid fertilizer is probably the easiest to use but be sure to dilute it sufficiently and feed mainly in the growing season. Suspend feeding during a very wet season as the growth will tend to be weak and sappy. Do not feed at all during the dormant season. Careful inspection of the trees at all times will soon bring a wider experience, and watering and feeding will appear less difficult.

Remember that watering, feeding and the types of compost used are all related to one another and all must receive careful attention if your trees are to remain healthy.

xvii — Elm
Imported by Bromage and Young Ltd. from Fukukaen Bonsai Nurseries, Nagoya, for Norman Gryspeerdt.

The age of this tree is unknown but with its ancient, hollow trunk it must be at least 50 years old. It will have been collected from the wild.

xviii — Rock grown Maple
Imported by Bromage and Young Ltd. from Fukukaen Bonsai Nurseries, Nagoya, for Norman Gryspeerdt.

This Trident Maple, which is thought to be about 30 years old will have been grown from a seedling or a cutting. It is a fine example of a rock grown tree with the gnarled roots running down the rock into the container. Its present height is 7".

ROCK-GROWN TREES

Ishi-tzuki (rock-grown trees) and group plantings require rather different treatment from the other styles and it will be less confusing to deal with all aspects of these bonsai in a separate section.

Rock-grown bonsai are probably the most interesting and arresting of all the styles of bonsai. The suggestion of landscape, the rugged grandeur of mountain top or stony plateau from which the tree springs, is typically Japanese. Again and again we see these scenes depicted in the delicate paintings from all periods of their history and to reproduce this landscape in miniature is the aim of every grower of rock bonsai.

This type of planting requires much patience and skill for success. Considerable thought should be given to the various aspects of the project before the initial planting. The suitability of all the material to be used should be assessed carefully. Plants, stones, subsidiary planting material and container should all blend together to produce a balanced and artistic creation. Thought should be given as to which type of planting suits the tree.

Cavity planting—in this case the tree is planted in a natural cavity in the rock which contains the roots and soil as does an ordinary container. Drainage may be effected by natural cracks in the rock or a little judicious drilling may enlarge the fissures. Unless badly mis-managed this, and the porosity of the rock, should provide enough drainage. The rock may stand on its own or in a container filled with water or sand.

Clasped to stone—here the plant is established on a stone but some of the roots lead down to the container which is filled with soil and has the usual drainage arrangements. The container must be in keeping with the height and breadth of the bonsai.

Slab planting—another method that should be mentioned, although it is not seen so often, is the planting of trees on a fairly flat slab of stone. Much care is required to produce the most suitable soil for this planting and after care must receive particular attention, it is fatally easy to wash away the soil with injudicious watering.

The choice of tree for rock-grown bonsai is very important. As with all bonsai it should have fine leafed foliage and be many branched, ezo spruce, chinese juniper and azaleas are all suitable and a very beautiful bonsai can be made with several of the acers. A young tree with a well grown root system is the best choice, an older tree will take longer to establish and will require expert care. I think it is best to take each type of ishi-tzuki separately to avoid confusing the different methods of planting. Plan to do this type of planting in the spring, the tree is then at its most vigorous and will struggle to re-establish itself.

CAVITY PLANTING

A cavity planted ishi-tzuki can be treated in the same way as a container planting. Drainage must be ensured, if the cavity does not drain naturally a drill may be used to provide sufficient outlet, also the cavity itself may be enlarged in this way. The exit of the drainage hole should be covered with vinyl mesh or crocks and a layer of gravel. The tree is prepared as for planting in a container, the roots are trimmed to promote fibrous growth and when repotting is necessary the trees can be removed and the roots trimmed again before fresh soil is added. More than one tree may be used for this type of planting and it is often possible to combine two types of trees; the main planting would be a spruce and smaller cavities filled with azaleas—which have the added advantage of flowering at certain times of the year.

If the bonsai stands outside a container is not necessary. The stone may stand, instead, on a bed of sand which will absorb the excess moisture which drains away after watering. For indoor displays a shallow container without a drainage hole or a tray

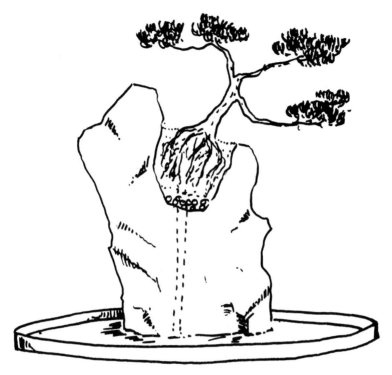

48 *Cavity planting shown in section.*

filled with sand or water provides a pleasant base. The reflection of the miniature landscape in the tray of water will be an added beauty particularly if a flowering shrub is used in the composition.

CLASPED TO STONE

For this style of bonsai a different approach is required. As before a young plant with a good root system is used but this time the roots must not be pruned. The long, trailing roots are required to run down the sides of the stone into the container below. When the stone and tree to be used have been selected choose, also, a container to fit the stone. The container must be

91

prepared as if to receive a plant, drainage holes are covered with mesh and the usual compost is added. The stone is placed on this first layer of soil, making sure that it sits firmly without rocking.

49   *Clasped to stone style.*

Wash the soil from the roots of the tree and separate them out as much as possible. The most useful shape of rock has a saddle or depression for siting the tree and the roots will lead from each side of this point into the container below.

A different mixture of soil is required on the rock itself. A sticky combination of soil, clay and peat is made and plastered on to the saddle and also down the rock where the roots are to run. When sufficient of this compost adheres to the rock the tree is placed firmly in position; the roots leading into the container are pressed into the soil and more of this mixture is put on top. The ends of the roots are arranged in the container and carefully covered with the usual bonsai compost. The roots running down the side of the stone may be tied in place with raffia until they have become established and then, on subsequent handling, very great care must be taken not to dislodge the plant from the stone. When repotting is necessary the stone and plant are treated as one and removed from the container and fresh soil is provided for the roots in the container. As the roots grasp the rock the soil covering them may be gradually washed away from them and, over the years, they will develop and a very fine effect can be achieved with the gnarled roots running down the sides of the rock to the container.

Where the rock has no obliging 'saddle' it is usual to provide fastenings to hold the plant to the rock. Wire loops may be fixed to the rock with one of the many adhesives on the market today and, when this has set, fine wires may be passed through the loops and used to tie the tree into place. These wires will be covered by soil and the plant will appear to be clinging to the rock; moss, pressed into the soil, will help to retain moisture and also indicate when the soil is drying out.

When planting is completed the after care will be important. The newly planted tree must be kept in the shade and out of the wind for some weeks so that the soil does not dry out too quickly or the tree shake in the wind and disturb the roots. The tree should be sprayed frequently, both the leaves and the roots will benefit. Excess water will drain away and you will be sure that sufficient moisture has been given. Rock plantings dry out very quickly and, once dry, the mixture used to plaster over the stone is very difficult to damp again. I cannot stress too much that the greatest attention should be paid to the watering of these bonsai in the months that they are becoming established.

SLAB PLANTING

Trees planted in this way appear to be rising from a rocky plateau and they present a number of problems. Drainage is not difficult of course, excess water will simply run off and unless there is a depression in the rock it will not collect and 'drown' the roots. As with the previous styles, one tree or several may be used for this planting and it is as well to fasten the trees on firmly, as described earlier, with wires. The soil should be the same sticky mixture that will adhere to the rock and a liberal amount should be placed on the slab in the first instance. The wires are threaded through the loops affixed to the slab and when the tree or trees are in position—roots carefully spread—they are fastened into

50   *Slab planting showing method of fastening.*

place. More soil is plastered over the roots and firmed gently; moss liberally applied and pressed into the soil will help to retain moisture and will also prevent the soil from washing away.

Once more, the greatest care must be taken to keep the soil moist and the moss will prevent evaporation to some extent. If you are in doubt scrape away a little of the moss very gently and examine the soil beneath. It is most important not to let the compost dry out as it is so difficult for water to penetrate this mixture of soil when it is really dry. If it should dry out, a very fine spray, applied gently to start with, is the best way to damp it again.

With slab plantings it is not possible to repot as the roots should not be detached from the rock. However, if renewed soil is necessary the moss should be removed and some of the old soil taken away and replaced with fresh compost of the same type. A tree planted on a slab may, after many years, need to be removed from the rock to a container to keep it healthy. The tree must be watched for signs of poor development and before any damage is done it can be taken off the rock and planted in an ordinary container.

This problem does not arise when the roots of the tree run down the sides of the rock into the container—in this case the roots can be nourished in the ordinary way and the bonsai can be repotted periodically. This is, therefore, a more permanent ishi-tzuki and when really established can be very impressive with the gnarled roots grasping the rock.

GROUPS OF TREES

This is a popular form of bonsai planting. A group of trees planted in a container to represent the forests, woods or groves that are found in nature can be a source of great interest and pleasure the year round. The trees used may be evergreen or deciduous or a combination of both; although great care is required in composing the planting if both deciduous and ever-green trees are used and the maintenance of the group is likely to be difficult. A group planting of this type must not be confused with the apparent groups of trees that are root connected. The root connected groups are, in effect, one tree and as such are easier to care for than a group composed of separate trees.

xix — Trident Maple Group
Imported in 1966 by Bromage and Young Ltd. from Fukukaen Bonsai Nurseries, Nagoya, for Norman Gryspeerdt.

This apparent group of trees is a raft planting and is reputed to be 40 years old. It has been grown from a single root of a seedling or a cutting and its present height is 28″.

xx — Group of Elms
Imported by Bromage and Young Ltd. from Fukukaen Bonsai Nurseries, Nagoya.

These Elm trees, imported individually over a period of three years, were arranged in their present grouping by Norman Gryspeerdt in 1965. He estimates the age of the trees as between 10 and 20 years. The height of the group is under 8″ although when in leaf it will appear a little taller.

The advantage of this type of planting for a beginner is that young trees may be used and a bonsai of finished appearance can be created in a short time. The trunk of a single tree takes time to develop but the trunks of the trees of a group planting are not so thick—compare a specimen tree in a field with the trees of a copse and the difference will be immediately apparent.

Try, if possible, to choose seedlings or cuttings from the same parent tree for the trees of the group. The more nearly the trees of a group planting resemble one another the more unified the group will appear, although they should, of course, be of different sizes so that an interesting and natural group may be planned. Seedlings will develop at different rates and when the few required for single tree styles have been chosen the remainder may be just what is needed to make a good group planting.

Certain species of trees are more suitable for group planting than others and they should be chosen for small leafed foliage and for roots that will tolerate severe pruning. It is not usual to see flowering trees in a group planting, the number of trees detracts from the beauty of the flowers and the species are usually difficult to maintain in a group.

The container used for yose-ue (group planting) is of great importance. It can be oval, round or rectangular but it must be shallow in proportion to its surface area. This gives the illusion of distance at ground level and an impression of height with regard to the trees. Drainage is the same as for all bonsai containers and vinyl mesh is better, in this instance, than crocks because of the relatively shallow container. The compost used for a yose-ue is the same as that for a single container grown tree.

Spring is the best season for creating a group planting as the roots often require considerable pruning due to the lack of depth in the container; the growing period which follows will see the trees producing new fibrous roots to replace those removed.

97

To obtain the very best possible results, have to hand a larger number of trees than you require so that the most suitable may be chosen to compose the group. The informal appearance of a good yose-ue is deceptive, the composition will have been studied with great care so that unnatural symetry is avoided. A style much used by the Japanese is based on a 'family' design. As with a sokan bonsai, where the larger trunk represents the parent and the smaller trunk the child, the group plantings may consist of 'grandparents', 'parents' and 'children'. The 'grandparent' will be the focal point while the 'parents' are the secondary interest

51   *'Family' design — older members of family represented by larger trees.*

and the 'children' make up the unity of the group by careful positioning.

An interesting arrangement can be achieved by planting a large tree to the front of the container and smaller ones to the back—this gives an impression of distance and perspective. A composition in a large container will benefit from a difference in surface levels so that part of the terrain is higher and represents the rolling hills of a landscape. A study of trees in natural surroundings will show that the space between the trees is as important to the composition as the location of the trees themselves. The illusion of the depths of the forest or that of groups of trees scattered on a plain can be created by the careful placing of the trees relative to space.

52   *Group planting using different surface levels.*

Preparing the soil and container for planting a group of trees is very much the same as for a single tree. Roots will need considerable trimming and if a large proportion has been removed reduce the top of the tree correspondingly. Do not begin to plant until the complete scheme has been planned or confusion will result and a good bonsai will not be achieved.

Sometimes there is difficulty in persuading the trees to remain in place. You can use heavier moistened soil at the roots to hold them firm but there is a danger of excluding air. I prefer to wire the trees into place and use dry soil for planting. Position the wires so that they may be removed when the trees no longer require support.

Water the planting gently but thoroughly when it is finished and leave it in a shaded, sheltered spot for some weeks. After the new roots have formed and the trees are firm the wires may be removed and any training may commence. When repotting the bonsai it should be done as a single unit without separating the trees. Any tree that no longer harmonises with the planting as a whole can be replaced at this time and the bonsai restored to the original design.

5

Situation and Display

For the owner of a single imported bonsai there is no problem of display. When the plant is indoors it stands in that part of the room that will present it at its best, while outdoors a favoured place filled with sunshine but sheltered is not too difficult to find. Complications arise when the collection grows—as it is bound to —and room must be found for fifty or a hundred trees.

Bonsai, by their very nature, are on display all the time and will demand your attention. When displaying one indoors you will find that it is just not possible to put it in a position where it is cluttered up with ornaments and bric-a-brac. Silently the tree demands the traditional treatment received in Japan. Simplicity of presentation is the answer. The traditional Japanese home is centred around the 'tokonoma' where would be placed a precious object of ceramic ware or bronze, a supremely simple flower arrangement in the Japanese style (ikebana), or a fine painted scroll. Those things that are held most desirable are displayed there, not so much for admiration as for contemplation. The buddhist philosophy hinges on contemplation and an aesthetically beautiful object acts as a centre of meditation. Our homes do not have a tokonoma but a simple stand or small table, placed in a good light against a plain background, will display a bonsai or a group of mame bonsai quite adequately. A collection of bonsai will enable you to retain the little display, changing the tree on the stand every few days so that no one tree remains too long indoors.

Out of doors the problem is to display a number of bonsai. Part of the garden or terrace can be set aside for this, depending on the size of the collection to be accommodated. Bear in mind that the trees need daily watering and the site chosen will need to be well drained. The stands should be built of hardwood and have several different levels, if possible, to show all the trees to the best advantage. Some shade should be provided from the heat of the sun; a construction of slatted wood supported on strong posts above the area would serve to break up the sunlight. Don't stand the bonsai under trees for shade, the dripping of the leaves during a rainy period would be very injurious. Choose a site out of the wind or erect a windbreak to shelter the trees. Bonsai standing on a windy site will not thrive and the young leaves of deciduous trees will be burned as effectively by the wind as by the sun. For your convenience, as well as pleasure, situate your bonsai 'centre' near the house. The trees require daily attention and this is easier to provide if they are conveniently placed.

Stands should be designed to cater specifically for the bonsai that you already have or those that you intend to grow. Larger trees will require sturdy shelves while a kengai (cascading) bonsai will need a high stall to show the tree to its best advantage. The stands must be constructed to allow water to drain away and the plants on the higher levels must not drain onto those lower down.

xxi and xxii — Garden Display
Norman Gryspeerdt displays his trees against a plain
background. They are protected by a slatted shade and are
at a comfortable height for observation and daily attention.

xxiii — Display of Containers
  These containers are imported from Japan. They show the
wide variety of shapes and sizes obtainable although the
whole range is not represented.

No bonsai should ever be allowed to stand on the ground, it will tend to harbour pests. If it is possible to present the trees against a plain background so much the better but, failing this, a paved area, somewhat larger than that of the shelves and stands, will provide a suitable setting for display. When planning the stands allow enough room for each tree so that they will not be too close together, bonsai must have a reasonable amount of space if they are to develop properly.

A nursery bed is a useful addition to your bonsai centre and a cold green-house or a large cold frame will be invaluable during the winter months; the danger of frost is everpresent. If your containers are frost proof at least they will not be damaged, but prolonged frost will mean that the trees will be deprived of moisture. Snow will do no harm as long as it is not allowed to accumulate and damage the branches.

CONTAINERS

I have deliberately refrained from saying a great deal on the subject of containers so far because I feel that it is more useful for the information to be centred in one section. An imported tree complete with pot presents no problem but there are a large variety of shapes, styles and colours (suitable and unsuitable) to choose from when buying containers for existing or future trees. It will not do to buy a pot because you like the colour—the important thing to consider is whether the container you are buying will make a unified whole when the tree, for which you are buying it, is planted. A collection of containers acquired gradually is of great value, this ensures that sufficient choice will be available and the best suited vessel may be used for each tree. Quiet, natural colours will be found to have the widest application.

Bonsai containers must conform to certain standards if the tree is to remain healthy. In the first place there must be adequate

105

drainage. A rectangular pot with an inside measurement of six inches by three inches will have two drainage holes three quarters of an inch in diameter, while a round pot five inches in diameter will have a one inch drainage hole. To those accustomed to ordinary flower pots this may seem excessive but the correct drainage is essential for these trees. To allow the waste water to run away rather than be trapped under the pot the container is raised on feet so that there is a space of at least a quarter of an inch between the base of the container and the surface upon which it is standing. There are containers for sale without drainage holes, they are usually very shallow and are suitable for ishi-tzuki where the bonsai are grown on the rock and the container is used as a display vessel only. Water or sand is kept in the container as a base for the stone and will serve to hold any moisture that drains off the rock during watering.

Containers may be glazed or unglazed. If they are glazed it should only be a partial glaze extending from the inside of the top rim to the bottom edge of the outside of the container, leaving the larger part of the inside and the whole of the base of the container unglazed. Pots that are completely unglazed are considered the best but for indoor display in particular the glazed container can add considerably to the appearance of the bonsai, although the subdued colours of the unglazed containers are well suited to evergreen trees.

The second important consideration is the frost proof quality of the containers. Many bonsai are completely hardy and should remain outside for the greater part of the year. This being the case it is, of course, important that the container should be frost resistant. Some containers made in this country are not suitable from this point of view. A frost proof pot is reasonably thick and is made of the same type of clay and fired to a similar temperature as an oven-proof culinary dish. At the moment there are more imported pots of the correct standard than those made in this country but the growing demand will, no doubt, soon bring the supply.

It is quite an expensive business to provide 'honbachi' (a real bonsai pot) for a large collection of trees but, if you are able to keep the trees free of frost in winter there is no reason why unglazed seed pans, which come in various sizes, should not be used. Terracotta saucers—used under flower pots—may be drilled quite easily to provide sufficient drainage and should stand on slatted shelves to allow the water to drain away completely. Some firms make pans for growing alpine plants and these are also suitable for bonsai but do remember that they will not withstand frost.

Occasionally it is possible to use some vessel with a pleasing appearance which was not originally made as a container. If this is the case it will probably be glazed inside and out. Drilling must be carried out with great care to obtain sufficient drainage; even so only shallow vessels of this type are suitable, the glazing does not allow the pot to 'breathe' and the soil in a deeper pot will quickly become stagnant and sour. It is safest, particularly for the beginner, to rely on the correct container or the unglazed pottery pans.

The size and style of a tree, or group of trees, will have much to do with the choice of container. Many different sizes and shapes are available and the correctly proportioned container will enhance the beauty of the bonsai. Usually containers are shallow in relation to the surface area although with some styles, kengai or cascading for instance, a deeper pot is used to balance the shape of the tree. Very shallow containers are used for group plantings and in every type of planting the pleasing proportion of height and width of tree to container should be considered. Try to see as many good bonsai as possible at exhibitions and at nurseries where they import large numbers; photographs of bonsai masterpieces are also helpful in developing an 'eye' for the relation of vessel to tree. The finished picture must be harmonious and artistic and the volume of the pot should suggest the great height, girth and age of the tree.

Glazed vessels come in a variety of colours and here, again, you must use good judgement. Natural clay colours, brown, grey, black and subdued red, are perhaps the best of all; they do not obtrude upon the eye but form a pleasing background for the tree. There are no hard and fast rules but avoid garish colours, green should blend, not clash, with the foliage and the container should contrast with, not try to match, the colour of the blossom. So, the most important consideration is that the container should complement the tree rather than compete with it for attention. Although the correct container is very important to the health of the tree and also to its appearance, it should be the last thing about the bonsai to catch the eye. The order of attention should be:—

What a lovely tree.

How is it planted.

That's a good container.

STONE

There are various uses for stone in the art of bonsai. Stone chippings may cover the surface of the ground for the purpose of moisture retention or a few pieces may be used for decorative effect. The stone must be natural and not the rather highly coloured pieces found in some garden sundries shops; these, no doubt, have their place but they are not for bonsai.

Larger stones can be strategically set on the surface, after repotting, to hold the roots in place. Where a tree has been planted on a slant, for instance, a stone can be so placed as to prevent the roots from pulling out of the ground before the new roots have begun to grow and give stability. This can be of great assistance where a group planting has been designed; the trees may have been severely root pruned and a few carefully positioned stones will keep them upright and in place until their own roots are able to do so. These stones, if well chosen, will look like part of the landscape and should all be of the same type with the grain running in the same direction.

Rock grown bonsai call for larger pieces. These should be of varied and interesting shape and should have a firm, flat base to avoid any movement which, after planting, would tend to disturb the roots of the tree. Pumice or tufa stone is used also sandstone and granite of which many useful pieces can be found without difficulty. Do not, however, use stones found on the seashore as these will be impregnated with salt and will harm the tree. Stone from a river bed is suitable but will probably have become too smooth; a rugged stone gives the impression of a natural landscape. Sometimes a vein of quartz will be found running down a rock, when planted and placed for display it will appear to be a waterfall issuing from the rocky landscape. When choosing stone remember that it will have to be moved from time to time and don't use one that will be too heavy.

Hard stone is longer lasting—the wisdom of the choice is seen in some of the fine old bonsai planted on stones many decades ago. The advantage of softer stone is that it can be altered fairly easily if the shape is not quite suitable; channels can be filed for roots, cavities and drainage holes may be enlarged and the base flattened if the stone is not sufficiently stable. Granite and sandstone will probably be found the most suitable for slab plantings although sandstone may tend to laminate in the frost. Where a plant is to be held to a rock with wire and there is little in the way of natural depressions, a rough textured rock is to be

109

preferred so that the sticky, clay-peat mixture will cling to it more easily.

When choosing rock for an ishi-tzuki treat it as a container and consider it from all angles so that the most interesting face of the rock is to the 'front' and the shape and colour of the rock suit the tree with which it is to form a bonsai. As with containers, try to have a selection to hand so that when you require a stone or stones for a composition there will be several from which to choose.

TOOLS

Under this heading comes the list of odds and ends that make a gardeners' life easier. Some of them will not be tools in the strictest sense of the word and others will be found in the culinary department rather than in the gardening section. To this list I am sure you will add your own indispensible items.

Watering. A small can with a long spout is essential. The can may be used without a rose for watering the soil and with a fine rose for the foliage. One of my aids for watering is a small plastic bottle with a fitting that allows a fine spray to be directed by simply squeezing the bottle. This is most useful for watering rock grown bonsai, keeping moss damp and for cleaning the leaves. I also use a larger, more conventional spray, with a pumping action, which gives a fine, wide mist for the foliage.

Potting and Repotting. In Japan nests of seives are used for grading the compost but it is possible to find a variety of mesh sizes and these will serve very well. A turntable is useful in many ways and saves possible damage when one of the larger bonsai must be turned about for root trimming and so forth. They are sold specifically for this purpose in Japan but a culinary icing table or a home-made wooden turntable, like my own, is quite as successful. For removing trees from pots a piece of dowelling, cut straight across and sandpapered smooth, is a handy tool. Pushed up into the drainage hole slowly but firmly it will loosen the tree and make it easy to remove from the container—it would be very injurious to try to dig the tree out from the top, or to pull it out by the trunk, without first loosening the whole.

There are a variety of small trowels etc. on the market and one or two of these would be a worthwhile investment. The stainless steel ones being the best. One of my most treasured implements is a two pronged fork made by filing off the two outer prongs of an old fork; it isn't too sharp and is very good for removing the soil around the outside of the root ball before trimming the roots. A wooden skewer will probe the root ball and also help to settle the soil in the container while filling with fresh compost.

A fine vinyl mesh is one of the best methods of screening the drainage hole, crocks may be used in the deeper containers but with a shallow one the mesh is preferable as it takes up less room. Thorough cleaning of the containers is important and small scrubbing brushes will be found suitable, for the smaller containers a round bristle scourer, with a long handle, as used in the kitchen is ideal.

Training. Copper wires of varying thickness and fine vinyl covered wire or pipe cleaners for delicate shoots, are the most practical. If the bark is easily marked it may be necessary to wind the wire, or the branch, with raffia. Raffia is also used for tying two branches closer or tying a bamboo or dowelling splint to a trunk. Weights, as used by fishermen, are also used in training and many prefer this method to wiring. Various tools are required for pruning and must be kept sharp and clean, secateurs for the larger branches and roots and sharp scissors for trimming small roots and shoots. Fine scissors are best for leaf trimming where this is carried out. Pliers will be needed for removing wire used in training—the wire will be harder after use than when putting

111

it in place soon after annealing. Wire cutters will also be required. A pruning knife is the best for taking cuttings, shaping the stock and scion of grafts and making the necessary cuts when layering; it should also be used where a branch must be taken off very close to the trunk or a natural looking snag is to be formed from a stump.

Polythene (bags or sheeting) is used to prevent loss of moisture when lifting a plant from the wild or when propagating. The various items for propagation are quite simple, pots, pans and boxes—all clean and well drained—peat pots, suitable composts, hormone powder, labels and any other equipment that you have always used in propagating.

RECORDS

A practical contribution to a bonsai growers' knowledge is a set of records. Obviously it would not be possible to keep detailed case histories of a large collection, and collections have a habit of becoming larger than was at first intended, but I have found that photographs taken at yearly intervals and notes relating to them of great interest. The bonsai is there, of course, and speaks for itself, but to know how it appeared ten years ago is a matter for the record. Looking back over even a few years will show the success, or otherwise, of the treatment accorded to a certain tree. The memory is not infallible and exaggerates or denigrates according to ones' nature.

When considering the training of a recently acquired tree it can be most helpful to recall the pruning, trimming and wiring used on another occasion and to evaluate the result. A beginner, in particular, although he follows advice, does so in ignorance of the eventual outcome. Passing years bring greater experience with his hobby but to say with certainty 'I obtained this result with that method' is better than to say 'I think I obtained this result with that method'. Theory is one thing but practise, and a description of the processes used noted down for future reference, brings greater certainty of the methods best suited to any particular tree.

A photographic record, taken once a year, and a note or two cn the back of each print is often sufficient. Then choose one or two trees of each species, possibly of differing styles, and keep a more detailed summary of treatment and reaction. It is useful to know where and when you obtained the tree and its appearance at that time (height and so on), the subsequent treatment and comments on its success. Illustrated by photographs, or possibly diagrams, these thumbnail sketches will provide a surprising amount of information which, gathered bit by bit, is of great value when assembled in an orderly form.

6

Suitable Species

The following section deals with species considered suitable for bonsai culture. Many are imported from Japan while others have been pioneered as bonsai by English growers. The list is by no means complete and any tree or shrub that appears to have possibilities as a bonsai is worth growing. These notes are brief and I would suggest a little general research into soil required, growth habits etc., if you are trying out a species unfamiliar to you. The more information that you can gather on the general characteristics of the plant the greater will be the chance of success when growing it as a bonsai.

I have tried to give a guide as to the possibilities of obtaining the various species mentioned, their description, treatment and suitability of style. The repotting and root pruning varies with the age of the plant and should only be undertaken after inspection. Older plants do not require repotting each year and many will remain quite safely for ten years in the same container and soil—but in this event do not neglect to feed the tree. Young trees will almost always need yearly repotting until the root system has sufficient fibrous roots to support the tree in a small container, usually where the tree is annually repotted feeding will not be necessary.

EVERGREENS

Abies (Fir), *A.procera, A. nobilis.*
   Specimen tree of great beauty. Trunk wide at base, tapers sharply. Short needles.
   Propagation by seed. Young stock obtainable in this country.
   Style. Suited to formal, upright styles. Single planting. Exposed root.
   Repot and root prune yearly. Good loam. Sufficient water. Feed monthly May to September.
Cedrus (Cedar), *C.deodara, C. libani, etc.*
   Good specimen tree. Trunk thick at base. Short needles. Horizontal branching.
   Propagation by seed. Young stock obtainable in this country.
   Style. Suited to formal upright or slanting. Single planting.
   Repot when necessary. Care required, some cedars shed needles (which are replaced later) after repotting. Sufficient water. Well drained soil.
Chamaecyparis (False Cypress), *C.obtusa, C.pisifera, etc.*
   Variety of forms—slender, bushy, slow growing—and foliage colour. Very small leaves.
   Propagation by seed or cuttings.
   Style. Various. Single planting, rock planting, exposed root.
   Repot and root prune yearly. Sandy soil. Sufficient water. Tolerates pruning and wiring well.
Cryptomeria japonica (Japanese Cedar).
   Evergreen but foliage turns bronze in autumn. Small leaved. Not always hardy.

115

Propagation by seed. Very easy by cuttings. Obtainable in this country. Imported from Japan.

Style. Single planting. Upright, slanting. Root connected.

Repot and root prune yearly. Trim shoots regularly—with fingers, may not tolerate metal. Prune larger branches in spring. Water copiously, spray. Feed monthly spring and autumn.

Juniperus (Juniper), *J.chinensis*, *J.rigida* (needle juniper) *J.squamata meyeri, etc.*

Small leaved. Very suitable for bonsai.

Propagation by cuttings. Obtainable in this country *J.chinensis* imported in large numbers from Japan.

Style. Very varied. Single and multiple plantings. Single and multiple trunk. Cascade, rock plantings.

Repot and root prune yearly in spring. Nip buds regularly with fingers. Prune and wire in spring. Water amply. Spray. Feed monthly spring and autumn. Tolerates lime.

Picea (Spruce), *P.glehnii* (Ezo), *P.sitchensis, etc.*

Fine needled foliage (Christmas tree type) Shallow rooted..

Propagation by cuttings. Some species obtainable in this country.

Style. Very varied. Single and group plantings. Single and multiple trunks. Rock plantings, exposed root.

Repot and root prune spring or autumn. Nip shoots frequently. Prune and wire in winter. Water well. Feed spring and autumn.

Pinus (Pine), *P.densiflora* (red pine), *P.mugo*, *P.thunbergii* (black pine), *P.sylvestris* (scots pine), *P.parviflora* (white pine).

Japanese symbol of life, much used for bonsai. May be two, three or five needled.

Propagation by seed or grafting. Collect from wild. Obtainable in this country. Imported from Japan.

Style. Various. Single and multiple planting. Rock planting and **raft.**

Repot and root prune frequently when young. Remove buds completely or trim when they are half grown. Prune branches in late autumn or early spring. Feed mainly in spring. Restrict water when needles are growing or they get too long. Spray. Well drained soil.

Sequoia (Redwood), *S.sempervirens, S.giganteum.*
Small needles, fibrous bark.
Propagation by seed.
Style. Single planting, upright.
Repot and root prune yearly in late spring or early autumn. Well drained soil. Water sufficiently. Prune with caution.

Taxus (Yew)
Scarlet berries. Dark green or golden foliage. Hardy. Trunk gives aged appearance as tree develops.
Propagation by seed (poisonous to humans) which should be stratified. Can be found in the wild. Obtainable in this country.
Style. Single planting. Multiple trunk. Rock or exposed root.
Repot and prune yearly in late spring. Train early summer and autumn. Feed April and May. Water sufficiently. Tolerates pruning well.

Thuja (Red Cedar), *T.orientalis, T.plicata.*
Fine foliaged tree.
Propagation from seed or cuttings.
Style. Single planting, upright trunk.
Repot and root prune May or September. Nip shoots in spring. Prune in autumn. Well drained soil. Water sufficiently. Tolerates lime.

Tsuga (Western Hemlock)
Small leaved. Good specimen tree. Downward sloping branches.
Propagation by seed. Obtainable in this country.
Style. Single and group plantings. Rock and exposed root.
Repot and root prune yearly. Well drained sandy soil. Trim

long shoots back to about one inch. Prune and wire in autumn. Will tolerate considerable pruning.

DECIDUOUS

Acer (Maple), *A.buergerianum*, *A.palmatum*, *A.p.atropurpureum*. Delicate trees with fine foliage. Good autumn colouring. Propagation by seed, cuttings, layers. Obtainable in this country. Imported from Japan.

Style. A large variety of styles. Single and multiple plantings. Clasped to stone, exposed root.

Repot and root prune yearly in early spring. Water well. Trim shoots at second node. Leaf trim in early summer. Wire with care while branches are supple. Do not over feed. Shade from sun and wind, burns easily.

Betula (Birch), *B.japonica*, *B.pendula alba*.

Small foliage, white or silver bark. Graceful tree.

Propagation by seed. Obtainable in this country.

Style. Single or group plantings. Single or multiple trunked.

Repot and root prune yearly in spring. Well drained soil. Water well. Spray. Shelter from strong sunlight. Nip shoots back to two or three nodes until June. Wire when supple.

Carpinus (hornbeam), *C.laxiflora*.

Interesting trunk shape. Pretty bark. Catkins in spring. Attractive foliage in spring and autumn.

Propagation by seed—allow eighteen months for germination. Obtainable in this country. Imported from Japan.

Style. Multiple plantings and multiple trunk most suitable.

Repot and root prune yearly in early spring. Good loam. Water well. Feed in spring and autumn. Trim buds before they open. Wire in winter.

Fagus (Beech), *F.crenata*, *F.sylvatica*.

Spring foliage pale green. Russet brown leaves retained through winter. Fine trunk.

Propagation by seed. Found in wild. Obtainable in this country and imported (*crenata*).

Style. Single and multiple plantings. Good for groups. Rock and exposed root.

Repot and root prune yearly in spring. Good loam. Water well. Shade from sun and wind. Spray. Trim shoots early to second node. Leaf trim in June. Wire when supple. Feed sparingly.

Ginkgo biloba (Maidenhair tree).

Two lobed, fan shaped leaves, green in summer and yellow in autumn. Thick trunk. Much favoured for bonsai.

Propagation by cuttings. Difficult from seed. Obtainable in this country. Imported from Japan.

Style. Single upright planting. Exposed root.

Repot and root prune yearly in spring. Well drained soil. Prune when repotting. Trim in spring. Water well. Should not require wiring.

Quercus (Oak).

Attractive leaves, particularly when first out. Much branched in form. Good for bonsai.

Propagation by seed. Seedlings in wild.

Style. Single plantings or group. Single or multiple trunk. Rock grown, slanted or twisted forms.

Repot and root prune in early spring. Well drained soil. Sufficient water. Prune when repotting. Trim shoots to two or three nodes. Wire in summer.

Salix (Willow), *S.helvetica* (weeping), *S.repens* (creeping).

Weeping variety much prized.

Propagation by cuttings, layers and division. Obtainable in this country. Imported from Japan.

Style. Single or multiple plantings. Cascade.

Repot and root prune in early spring, examine in autumn — it may need repotting again. Trim back shoots when repotting.

Wire in early summer, wrap shoots. Water copiously.

Tilia (Lime), *T.cordata.*

Attractive red twigs, small pale green, heart shaped leaves.

Propagation by seed — allow two years. Layers and division. Obtainable in this country.

Style. Single and multiple trunk. Upright.

Repot and root prune yearly in spring. Good loam. Water well. Prune in autumn. Spray leaves.

Zelkova (Elm), *Z.serrata* (grey bark), *Z.ulmus parviflora.*

Small elm-like leaves. Good trunk with interesting roots at base. Fan shaped.

Propagation by seed. Imported from Japan.

Style. Single upright or group planting.

Repot and root prune yearly in spring. Good sandy loam, well drained. Sufficient water. Remove unwanted shoots at all times. Leaf trim in June. Prune to improve shape after the leaves have fallen. Do not leave wire on for long.

FLOWERING AND FRUITING

Akebia quinata.

Fragrant racemes of purple flowers in May. Deep green oval leaves, five to a stalk.

Propagation by seed.

Style. Various single plantings. Cascade.

Repot and root prune yearly in April. Well drained soil. Water sufficiently. Spray. Shelter from the wind. Remove unwanted shoots as they appear. Wire in June (weighting is best). Feed in summer.

Ardisia crenata (Kumquat).

Evergreen. White flowers, red fruits. Not hardy.

Propagation by seed or cuttings. Obtainable in this country.

Style. Various single plantings.

Repot and root prune in late spring. Good loam. May need phosphorous. Shade from full sun and wind. Shorten shoots in June. Prune in autumn.

Azalea and Rhododendron.

There is a considerable number of small flowered azaleas and rhododendrons that are suitable for bonsai. Propagation by cuttings. Obtainable in this country. Imported from Japan.

Style. Single and multiple planting. Single and multiple trunks. Cascade and clasped-to-stone.

Repot and root prune yearly after flowering. Moss is mixed with sandy loam. Sufficient water, more if exposed to full sun which is preferred. Protect from frost. Nip shoots to two or three leaves. Wire older plants with great caution, always cover wire. Spray and shade after repotting.

Berberis (barberry), *B.thunbergii, B. atropupurea.*

Small leaves, green or purple. Golden flowers. Very suitable for bonsai.

Propagation by seed or cuttings. Obtainable in this country. Style. Single planting. Single and multiple trunk.

Repot and root prune yearly in March. Water well. Leaf spray. Feed spring and early autumn. Remove shoots constantly.

Camellia, C.japonica, C. sasanqua.

Small flowered varieties are suitable. Glossy, evergreen leaves. Pink or white flowers.

Propagation by cutting and layers. Some suitable species may be obtainable in this country.

Style. Single planting. Single and multiple trunks.

Repot and root prune yearly in April or autumn — depending on time of flowering. Well drained soil with peat. Water sufficiently. Full sun. Prune when repotting. Trim shoots in July taking care to leave flower buds for the following year. Train in early summer, wire cautiously with wrapped wire.

121

Chaenomeles speciosa (Japanese quince).

Scarlet blossom in March. Deciduous.

Propagation by seed, cuttings, layers and division. Obtainable in this country and imported from Japan.

Style. Single planting. Cascade, raft and rock-grown.

Repot and root prune yearly in autumn. Well drained soil. Water sufficiently. Trim shoots in June. Prune in autumn. Do not allow too much fruit to develop. Spray only when repotted.

Chimonanthus fragrans (Winter sweet).

Pale primrose flowers in winter. Not hardy.

Propagation by layers. Obtainable in this country.

Style. Single plantings, various forms.

Repot and root prune in early autumn. Well drained soil. Water sufficiently. Prune in early summer. Shade from sun. Do not wire in winter, branches are brittle then.

Cornus mas (Cornelian cherry).

Small yellow clusters of flowers in February. Red, oval fruit. Deciduous.

Propagation by seed, layers or division. Obtainable in this country.

Style. Single planting, various styles. Single and multiple trunk.

Repot and root prune yearly in early autumn. Prune at the same time. Do not overwater.

Corokia cotoneaster.

Small leaves, tiny yellow flowers. Twisted form of growth. Good for bonsai. Not hardy.

Propagation by cuttings. Obtainable in this country.

Style. Single planting. Single and multiple trunk.

Repot and root prune yearly in early spring. Well drained soil. Sufficient water. Full sun. Trim shoots in June. Should not require wiring.

Cotoneaster. C. horizontalis, C. microphyllus.
Many varieties. Deciduous and evergreen. Small leaves, flowers and fruit. Very suitable for bonsai.
Propagation by seed and half-ripe cuttings. Obtainable in this country. Imported from Japan.
Style. Single or multiple planting. Single or multiple trunk. Cascade and rock-grown.
Repot and root prune (if necessary) in autumn or spring. Well drained soil. Prune shoots in summer after flowering. Young wood does not retain shape if wired. Feed after fruiting. Some fruit should be removed to avoid weakening tree.
Crataegus (Hawthorn), *C. cuneata.*
Small leaves. Bright flowers and fruits. Deciduous.
Propagation by seed, after stratifying. Grafting. Obtainable in this country.
Style. Single planting. Single trunk. Slanting, cascade.
Repot and root prune yearly in early spring. Well drained soil. Water sufficiently. Trim shoots in June. Wire in summer, wrapped. Remove some fruit.
Elaeagnus multiflora (Oleaster or Wild olive).
Small flowers and fruit. Deciduous, some evergreen.
Propagation by hardwood cuttings. Obtainable in this country.
Style. Single planting. Single and multiple trunk. Twisted, slanted and exposed root.
Repot and root prune yearly in late spring. Sandy soil. Water thoroughly. Prune when fruit forms. Wire as little as possible. Feed when fruit develops. Requires warmth in winter.
Euonymus (Spindle).
Many varieties both evergreen and deciduous. *E. alata* particularly good.
Propagation by cuttings or seed. Obtainable in this country.
Style. Single planting. Cascade.

123

Repot and root prune yearly in spring. Well drained soil. Water sufficiently. Trim shoots after flowering. Do not wire.

Exochorda (Pearl bush).

Small white flowers in May. Hardy.

Propagation by half-ripe cuttings. Seed. Obtainable in this country.

Style. Various single plantings. Cascade.

Repot and root prune yearly in spring. Well drained soil. Water sufficiently. Sunny position sheltered from wind. Prune immediately after flowering—following years flowers borne on new wood.

Forsythia.

Small yellow flowers in early spring. Numerous varieties, some not hardy.

Propagation by ripe or half-ripe cuttings. Obtainable in this country.

Style. Various single plantings. Cascade.

Repot and root prune yearly in autumn. Good loam. Water sufficiently. Prune immediately after flowering to one or two leaves. Full sun.

Gardenia jasminoides.

White scented flowers. Evergreen. Not hardy.

Propagation by cuttings or grafting.

Style. Single planting.

Repot and root prune yearly in late spring or early autumn. Well drained soil. Water sufficiently. Full sun. Trim shoots in June. Prune, if necessary, in autumn. Difficult to wire young shoots.

Jasminum nudiflorum (Winter jasmine).

Small yellow flowers from November to February. Deciduous. Propagation by layering and half-ripe cuttings. Obtainable in this country. Imported from Japan.

Style. Single planting. Single and multiple trunk Cascade and rock-grown (cavity planted).

Repot and root prune yearly in September. Sandy soil. Water sufficiently. Trim after bloom falls. Prune in dormant season. Feed early summer and late autumn.

Lagerstroemia indica (Crape myrtle).

Small white or red flowers in late summer. Fine bark. Not hardy.

Propagation by seed.

Styles. Various single plantings.

Repot and root prune yearly in April. Good sandy loam. Water thoroughly. Trim after blooming. Wire (wrapped) in July. Feed in autumn if required.

Lycium (Boxthorn).

Small purple flowers, red berries.

Propagation by seed. Half-ripe or hardwood cuttings. Obtainable in this country.

Style. Single planting. Single and multiple trunks. Cascade.

Repot and root prune yearly in late spring. Very well drained soil. Water sufficiently. Trim shoots regularly. Prune in spring.

Magnolia. M.liliflora (obovata), *M. kobus.*

Above varieties most suitable but flowers and leaves rather large for bonsai.

Propagation by seed, layers. Obtainable in this country.

Style. Single plantings.

Repot and root prune as little as possible. If it is necessary, wait till blossom falls. Peat in soil. Water sufficiently. Trim shoots in June.

Malus (Crab apple), *M.halliana.*

Small red or white blooms in early summer. Small colourful fruit in autumn. A number of varieties very suitable for bonsai. Propagation by seed, grafting and cuttings. Obtainable in this country. Imported from Japan.

125

Style. Various single plantings.

Repot and root prune yearly in early spring. Fairly heavy soil. Prune shoots after flowers drop. Heavy pruning in dormant season. Water thoroughly. Sunny position.

Morus alba (The "silk worm" mulberry).

Many small flowers and dark green leaves. Form of tree very suitable for bonsai.

Propagation by seed and hardwood cuttings.

Style. Single, upright plantings.

Repot yearly in spring. Roots dislike pruning. Good loam. Water thoroughly. Prune in early spring. Trim shoots at about half an inch. Wire when repotting. Feed regularly in spring and early summer.

Osmanthus asiaticus.

Glossy evergreen leaves with small, sweet scented flowers. Not entirely hardy. Very good for bonsai.

Propagation by cuttings or layers. Obtainable (several species) in this country.

Style. Single planting. Slanting and upright.

Repot and root prune yearly in March. Well drained soil. Do not overwater. Shade from full sun. Trim shoots before mid-summer. Prune when repotting. Wire (wrapped) in June. Remove flowers one year in three to rest tree.

Prunus. P. mume (Apricot), *P. jamasakura* (Cherry), *P. persica* (Peach), *P. tormentosa* (Bushberry), *P. amygdalus* (Almond). There are a number of varieties of each species. Some, like the cherry, dislike pruning. Small leaved and small flowered varieties should be chosen. Apricot is perhaps the easiest to grow as bonsai.

Propagation by seed, grafts and occasionally suckers may be found. Obtainable in this country and some imported from Japan.

Style. A variety of single plantings. Gnarled trunk. Slanting. Occasionally multiple trunk.

Repot and root prune in spring or autumn (depending on the flowering season). Porous soil. Water sparingly to prevent sappy growth. Trim back to two nodes after flowering. Always bear in mind the following years' flowers. Wire in early summer—cherry abhors copper wire. Wrap all wire. Hang branches for preference. Pruning of both roots and top growth should be done with a very sharp implement. Feed in growing season.

Punica granatum (Pomegranate).

Decorative flowers and small fruit. Deciduous. Not hardy. Very good for bonsai.

Propagation by seed, cuttings of half-ripe wood and grafting. Obtainable in this country. Imported from Japan.

Style. Single planting. Single and multiple trunk. Raft.

Repot and root prune in late spring. Sandy soil. Sufficient water. Trim after blooming. Some fruit removed. Wire in summer.

Pyrus simonii (Pear).

Small white flowers before leaves appear. Fruit rather large for bonsai.

Propagation by seed, grafting and division.

Style. Single planting, upright.

Repot and root prune yearly in spring. Retain larger part of the soil when repotting. Water thoroughly when tree is in fruit. Trim in June.

Pyracantha (Firethorn).

Neat leafed deciduous tree. Red or yellow berries in autumn. Tiny white flowers in June.

Propagation by seed (stratification), half-ripe cuttings. Obtainable in this country. Imported from Japan.

Style. Single and multiple plantings. Single and multiple trunk.

Cascade and rock-grown.

Repot and root prune in spring. Well drained soil. Water sufficiently. Trim shoots early summer. Wire in summer. Heavy pruning in autumn. Tolerates sun or partial shade.

Robinia (False acacia).

Pinate leaves. Open branched. White, sweetpea-like flowers in summer. Good general shape for bonsai.

Propagation by division and seed. Obtainable in this country. Style. Single planting upright. Raft and ne-tsurani.

Repot and root prune in spring. Sandy soil. Water thoroughly. Trim shoots early. Sun and shelter from the wind.

Styrax japonica (Snowdrop tree).

Small white flowers in June. Very fine bonsai.

Propagation by layers in autumn. Obtainable in this country. Style. Upright single planting.

Repot and root yearly in late spring. Sandy loam. Water thoroughly. Trim after flowering. Prune in autumn. Sunny sheltered position.

Wisteria.

Pinate leaves. Long racemes of scented flowers in May and June. Very decorative.

Propagation by seed, layering and cuttings. Obtainable in this country. Imported from Japan.

Repot and root prune yearly in early spring. Rich soil. Trim shoots back to two nodes as they grow. Water copiously in spring and summer. Wire after June with covered wire. Prune after flowers wither.

Style. Single planting. Cascade, gnarled trunk and exposed root.

Index

Index *(continued)*

Index *(continued)*